UNDERSTAND AND WRITE

A COMPANION VOLUME

Understand and Write: Teacher's Handbook
by ROLAND HINDMARSH

UNDERSTAND AND WRITE

Tests and Exercises in
English Comprehension and Composition
at Secondary Entrance Level
for Schools in Africa

BY

ROLAND HINDMARSH
formerly Inspector of Schools, Uganda

CAMBRIDGE UNIVERSITY PRESS

Cambridge
London   New York   New Rochelle
Melbourne   Sydney

Published by the Press Syndicate of the University of Cambridge
The Pitt Building, Trumpington Street, Cambridge CB2 IRP
32 East 57th Street, New York, NY 10022, USA
296 Beaconsfield Parade, Middle Park, Melbourne 3206, Australia
P.O. Box 62, Ibadan, Nigeria
P.O. Box 30583, Nairobi, Kenya

First published 1965
Reprinted 1969, 1971, 1975, 1977, 1978, 1980, 1983

First printed in Great Britain at the University Press, Cambridge
Reprinted in Great Britain by the Alden Press Ltd, Oxford

ISBN 0 521 05271 8

PREFACE

The aim of this book is to give training in comprehension and composition to pupils at the Secondary Entrance level in African schools where English is used as a second language. In East, Central and Southern Africa it is likely to be found most useful in the final year of pre-secondary school, in preparing for the leaving examination. In West Africa the structure of the educational system will probably make the book most suitable during the first year of secondary school.

The vocabulary and structures used in this book are based on an analysis of the vocabulary and structures used in the first five pupil's books in the *New Oxford English Course for East Africa* by F. G. French, published by the Oxford University Press. The passages, with their tests and exercises, are arranged in three stages:

Stage I: Passages 1–6. These make use of the 1300 words used in Books 1–4 of the Oxford Course.

Stage II: Passages 7–18. These make use of the 1500 words used in Books 1–4 of the Oxford Course, together with the first half (chapters 1–10) of Book 5.

Stage III: Passages 19–24. These make use of the 1750 words used in Books 1–5 of the Oxford Course.

Schools in Nigeria should note that F. G. French's *New Oxford English Course for Nigeria*, Books 1–5, is closely similar to the East African course, the first four books being linguistically almost identical.

This book of passages and exercises has the following principal features, some of which are believed to be new for a book of this kind at this level:

(1) Great care has been taken to write each passage within a strictly controlled vocabulary. Any new words outside the Oxford Book vocabulary for a given stage and, as far as possible, any new usages or expressions, are introduced with examples *before*

the pupil begins reading the passage. For each reading passage, there are never more than six new items, some of which will already be known to the more advanced pupils.

(2) Every passage is written within a set of structures that matches the range and frequency of usage of structures found in the appropriate group of Oxford books.

(3) Twenty-one of the twenty-four passages have been written especially for this book. They deal with scenes and events which are either within the pupil's experience or within the grasp of his imagination. The other three passages have been rewritten from books by three African writers: Cyprian Ekwensi, Robert Wellesley Cole and Chinua Achebe.

(4) Three different kinds of exercise involving comprehension training are set on each passage:

(a) a multiple-choice test of five or more questions;
(b) a set of five or more questions requiring written answers in sentence form;
(c) a new kind of exercise designed to train pupils in English composition by encouraging them to write imaginatively about the material provided in the reading passages.

There are no exercises of vocabulary work with individual words and phrases, as it is held that this work belongs to a different teaching context.

(5) Emphasis is placed on how to think out and compose answers to comprehension questions of the kind described in 4 (b) above. Detailed instructions are given to students in a special foreword.

(6) A teacher's book is available to give further information and advice. Its contents include:

(a) the complete vocabulary lists for the 1300, 1500 and 1750 word levels;
(b) these vocabulary lists in classified form under parts of speech and sub-classified for nouns and verbs into areas of meaning, such as *Clothes and Personal Ornament* for nouns, or *State and Change of State* for verbs;
(c) a discussion of the structural basis on which the passages were written;

(d) further suggestions on how to handle the preliminary vocabulary, how to improve reading efficiency and how to handle the multiple-choice tests;

(e) an analysis of reproduced sample answers and solutions from pupils in African schools, with a discussion of how to mark and evaluate these;

(f) guidance on the pronunciation of all new words introduced, as well as of some other words frequently mispronounced by African pupils.

During the preparation of this book, sample passages and exercises were tried out in schools in East and West Africa, and the results marked and assessed. In the light of these tests, alterations and adjustments were made. The passages were also all seen and commented on by teachers with overseas experience, principally in Africa. I wish here to express my thanks to the schools and teachers concerned, and especially to Mr Robin Kesterton, formerly Senior English Tutor at Kyambogo Teacher Training College, Kampala, and to Miss Sheelagh Warren of Gayaza High School, Uganda.

R.H.

CONTENTS

TO THE PUPIL

How to use this book

If you are hoping to join a secondary school next year, or if you have recently joined one, you may find this book useful. It is meant to help you to understand and write English better. It does this by giving you training in English comprehension and composition.

I. *A short explanation*

This book has twenty-four sections. Each section is built up in the same way, around a reading passage. The reading passages are shorter and easier at the beginning of the book. They are longer and more difficult at the end of the book.

Here are some notes showing you how each section is built up, and how to use the various parts in each section:

1. Before you begin reading

This gives words and expressions you need for the passage. Study them, but do no writing.

2. Reading passage

This is written in clear English using words and patterns that you should already know. Read it twice, but do no writing.

3. Test your understanding

Questions are asked on the passage. Four possible answers are given for each question. You must choose the right one. Write no words in your answer. Just

I

write the number of the question and the letter of the answer: 1 C, 2 A, 3 D, and so on. Try to do all the questions.

4. Answer questions in writing

Questions are asked on the passage. Write answers to all of them in correct English sentences. It may help you to go through the following six steps as you answer each question:

(1) Study the question to find out exactly what it means.

(2) Think out the ideas that will make your answer correct and complete.

(3) Build up a correct English sentence in your mind to express some or all of these ideas. (Do not translate sentences from the vernacular into English.)

(4) Write out the sentence carefully, using the right punctuation.

(5) Read the sentence over to make sure it is right.

(6) If you have not answered the question completely, build up, write out and read over other sentences in the same way, until the question is fully answered.

5. Imagine and write

Exercises are set about the passage. Try at least two, but try more if you wish. These exercises are to help you in English composition. You have to use your imagination and add things to the passage. There is no quick way of explaining how to do exercises of this kind. Turn to pages 6–9 of the longer explanation. There you will find out what you have to do.

II. *A longer explanation*

Before you begin reading

(1) Read this section, making sure of the words and expressions it gives. Perhaps you have met some of them before. Study them again to see if you have been right about their meaning and about the way to use them.

(2) Do no writing for this section.

Reading passage

(1) You should read this passage in the way your teacher tells you. There are many good ways of doing this.

(2) One good way of reading a passage is to read it quickly once and then slowly and carefully the second time. You will need to read the passage twice. It is almost impossible to understand a passage fully after reading it only once.

(3) While you are reading, try to make pictures in your mind about the people and things in the passage. Try to see what they look like, what shape they have, what colours they have, how they move, and what there is around them. Try to make the pictures as correct as you can.

Test your understanding

(1) After you have read the passage in the right way, turn to this part. It is made up of five or more questions on the reading passage. For each question there are four answers shown in the book. Each of these answers has a letter A, B, C or D. Only one of these four answers is correct. You must choose the correct one. You do this by thinking out which of the four answers makes the best sense for the reading passage. Then you write down only the number of the question and the letter of

the answer you have chosen: for example, 1 C, 2 A, 3 D, and so on.

(2) Do not write any words in your answers.

(3) Do not choose your answer quickly. Think carefully about each of the four answers given in the book. Often you will see at once that one of them is wrong. Another one may be half right and half wrong. That will not be the correct answer. To decide between the two answers that are left, you will perhaps have to read again some part or parts of the reading passage. Remember that you must choose the answer that *makes the best sense for the passage*.

Answer questions in writing

(1) You will have to take much more time and trouble in answering the questions in this part than you do in answering the questions in *Test your understanding*. There are two reasons for this:

   (i) No answers are given in the book for you to choose from.

   (ii) You have to put your answer into words, and arrange these words in correct English sentences.

(2) In answering each question, you have two difficulties to conquer. The first is to get the right points and ideas for your answer. The second is to put these clearly and correctly in English. Let us look at them one by one.

(3) You cannot get your answer right if you have not understood the question correctly and completely. You should read each question twice, slowly. Think out what it means exactly. One good way of doing this is to ask yourself what the question does *not* mean. Ask yourself what the question is *not* about.

(4) Another important point is to look carefully at the way the question is asked. A question beginning with *Who* should not be answered in the same way as a

4

question beginning with *Why*. Study the differences between: *What was...*; *What were...*; *How did...*; *How far did...*; *For what reasons...*; *In what ways...*; *How often...*; *How long...*; *When....*

(5) When you have decided on the exact meaning of the question, think out the idea or ideas which should be in your answer. Make sure that these ideas will give the answer to the whole meaning of the question, and not just to part of the meaning.

(6) Your second difficulty is to put the ideas for your answer into correct English sentences. When you were collecting these ideas, you had some words in your mind to help you to think about the ideas. These words were either in English or in your mother tongue. If the words were in English, they were perhaps short phrases such as 'in the morning' or even single words such as 'afraid' or 'rain'. If the words were in your mother tongue, there were perhaps many more of them in your mind.

(7) Start with the words already in your mind. If the words are in English, build up a sentence around the phrase or the single word. Use one of the sentence patterns you have been taught. Do not use a pattern you are not sure about. Choose patterns that make short sentences. Remember that you are allowed to use two, three, or even more sentences in your answer to the question. Short sentences give clear answers. One long sentence may not make your meaning clear.

(8) If the words in your mind are in your mother tongue, be careful. Do not translate the words into English. Take the most important word, the word that really gives the idea for your answer. Translate that word into English. Now build up an English sentence around that word, using a sentence pattern you know well. If your answer contains several ideas, you may have to build up other sentences in the same way.

(9) Build each sentence in your head, and say it to yourself before you do any writing. If the sentence is very long, you will not be able to say it to yourself. This means that the sentence is too long. There are too many ideas in it. Say the first part of it in one sentence. Keep the rest for another sentence.

(10) While you are saying the sentence to yourself, make sure it is in correct English. As soon as you have made sure of this, write the sentence out carefully. Take care with the punctuation. Remember to begin with a capital letter, to put commas where they are needed, and to end with a full-stop. Do not try to use semi-colons or colons. They are too difficult to use correctly. When you have finished writing the sentence, read it over to make sure you have written it out correctly.

(11) Now go on to the next sentence in your answer. If you have finished the answer to that question, turn to the next question, and go through the same six steps. You will find these given in a few words on page 2.

Imagine and write

(1) When you answer the questions in *Test your understanding* and *Answer questions in writing*, you must make sure that your answers are correct and complete. You do this by thinking about what is exactly said or meant in the reading passage.

(2) When you do the exercises in *Imagine and write*, you cannot find everything you need for your answers in the reading passage. Some of it may be there. But you will also have to add something that you make up yourself. You cannot change what the passage says, but you must say *more* than the passage tells you. This means that you must use your imagination in a special way.

(3) The easiest way to explain this is by an example. Here is a short passage for you to read:

6

I soon began to think about what was to happen when we got home. There would be biscuits brought especially from England in square tins. There would be cakes, bread and, best of all, there would be Jollof rice. I thought of Jabez and other friends who would come to spend the day with us. I thought of the visits we would pay to other persons in our family to wish them a happy Christmas and to get little presents of fruit or sweets.

The next thing I knew was that I thought I was being bitten by ants. I woke with a start to find my grandmother was squeezing me with the ends of her fingers.

'Stand up, Ageh!' she whispered.

She had been trying to wake me up for some time. I did not like my punishment, but I noticed that two other boys were also standing.

I looked carefully around me and saw black faces everywhere raised in the direction of a man in a high box on a wall. He was talking about the baby Jesus. As he went on, I felt that I would like to stand in a high box too and talk to all the people.

(4) You have understood that the passage tells you about what happened in church on Christmas Day to a small boy called Ageh. Here are two exercises on this passage. They have been done to show how you can write about the passage and add things from your own imagination.

Imagine you are the grandmother and write about what you saw and heard and did in church.

In church I was sitting beside Ageh. I noticed that he was not listening to the words or the songs. But I thought that he was a small boy and that it did not matter. After a time I saw that he had fallen asleep. I squeezed his leg with the ends of my fingers. When he awoke, I told him to stand up. He looked around him and did not seem to be happy. Then he listened again to what was said and seemed to be interested. When everything was over, we left the church and walked home.

(5) In this exercise you have to imagine you are the grandmother. You write about what you saw and heard and did in church. Most of the answer tells again what we already know from the passage. But some new things have been added. The passage does not say that Ageh was not listening to the words and songs. The passage does not say that the grandmother did not try to make Ageh listen, because he was still small. These things have been added from the imagination. They fit into the story of the passage.

(6) Here is the second exercise:

Imagine you are Ageh and write about what you did that day after leaving church.

After leaving church, we all walked home. I ran some of the way, because I wanted to eat the biscuits. But I had to wait until my mother came. She opened the square tin and gave three biscuits to me and to each of my brothers and sisters. Then Uncle Jabez and some other friends arrived and we had a meal of Jollof rice. I like Jollof rice very much. We always have it on Christmas day. In the evening when it was cooler, we visited Uncle John and Aunt Polly. We wished them a happy Christmas and they gave us fruit and sweets

8

to eat. But I was not very hungry. At sunset we walked home and I went to bed.

In this exercise you are Ageh and you are writing about what happened after church. You know something about this from Ageh's thoughts before he fell asleep. But you may add other things too, if you wish. The answer to this exercise adds that Ageh ran part of the way home and had to wait, that he had brothers and sisters, and that the relatives they visited were called Uncle John and Aunt Polly.

1   THE GEOGRAPHY TEST

Before you begin reading

Study these words:

homework: school work which you must do at home

> *Many children find it difficult to do their* **homework,** *because they do not have good lamps at home.*

to flow: to move along in the way a river moves

> *In the rainy season rivers usually* **flow** *more quickly than in the dry season.*

narrow: opposite of 'wide'

> *Many village paths are too* **narrow** *for a car to pass along them.*

second: one-sixtieth of a minute

> *Not very many men can run one hundred yards in less than ten* **seconds.**

Reading passage

From his seat, Oyoo could see that Ondieki had opened his geography book inside his desk and was trying to read all the chapter again as quickly as possible. Mutyaba was taking out his atlas and putting it on his desk.

5   'No geography books on the desks,' called out the

teacher, standing at the front. He took Mutyaba's atlas and put it on the teacher's table. 'Are you all ready?'

The boys held their pens ready and looked up at Mr Angwenyi.

'Question One. Write down the name of the longest river in Africa which flows towards the north.'

Oyoo saw all the boys' heads bend down over their desks. He looked at the narrow piece of paper in front of him. Nothing was written on it except 'Frederick Oyoo', '7B, 4/11/64'. He had read about a big river called the Congo, in a country far away to the west. He wrote on his paper: '1. River Congo'.

'Question Two. Write down the names of two African countries which grow a lot of cotton.'

This time Oyoo saw that many boys were unable to answer. Ondieki was trying to lift the lid of his desk, but Mr Angwenyi looked at him and he took his hands away. Mutyaba turned his head towards the window and seemed unhappy. Oyoo wrote '2. Uganda' on his paper. In his own country not much cotton was grown. Mr Angwenyi was going to read the next question. When he began speaking, Oyoo wrote 'Russia' quickly on his paper beside 'Uganda'.

'Question Three. In the north of Africa there is a large desert. Name it.'

Oyoo thought for a few seconds and put '3. Sahara' on his piece of paper. There were two more questions. Then the boys in the front desks walked to the back of the class, collecting the test papers. When Mutyaba reached the back of the class, Oyoo whispered to him: 'Easy questions today.'

When the papers were marked, Ondieki had four
answers correct and had scored eight marks. Oyoo had
40 three marks and Mutyaba four. Three boys had full
marks and seven had scored nine. Nobody had less than
three.

Test your understanding

1. The class were having
   A. a test of ten questions.
   B. a handwriting test.
   C. a geography test.
   D. a dictation test.

2. Mutyaba was sitting
   A. in one of the front desks.
   B. near Ondieki.
   C. behind Oyoo.
   D. somewhere in the middle of the class.

3. Oyoo scored nothing for Question One
   A. because he was too slow.
   B. because the Congo is not a long river.
   C. because the Congo is not in Africa.
   D. because the Congo does not flow north.

4. Oyoo scored only one mark for Question Two
   A. because no cotton is grown in Uganda.
   B. because no cotton is grown in Russia.
   C. because he had written 'Russia' badly.
   D. because Russia is not in Africa.

5. When Oyoo had answered Question Three, the
   number of words written on his paper was
   A. six.

B. seven.

C. three.

D. eight.

6. Oyoo's answers to Questions Four and Five

   A. were both wrong.

   B. were both right.

   C. were right for Four and wrong for Five.

   D. were wrong for Four and right for Five.

7. When the test was over, Oyoo

   A. pretended to Mutyaba that he had done quite well.

   B. was very unhappy.

   C. helped to collect the test papers.

   D. was very tired.

8. In the test, Oyoo

   A. had done quite well.

   B. had done badly.

   C. knew nearly as much as Ondieki.

   D. was nearly the weakest in his class.

9. Class 7 B did the test

   A. in April.

   B. in January.

   C. in November.

   D. at the end of November.

10. Oyoo came from

   A. Uganda.

   B. Russia.

   C. the Congo.

   D. a country not named in the passage.

Answer questions in writing

1. Write out everything that Oyoo had written on his paper when he had finished answering Question Three.

2. Say what each boy in 7 B had to do when Mr Angwenyi gave a geography test, before the first question was read out.

3. Write out everything you know from the passage about Ondieki.

4. Write down two things which show that Mutyaba was sitting at the front of the class.

5. How many marks were given for each correct answer? If Mutyaba got the first and third answers right, how did he get on with the other questions?

Imagine and write

1. Think of a subject in which you sometimes have tests at school. What do you have to do at the beginning of the lesson before you begin answering the first question of the test?

2. Write three sentences about things you can see and three sentences about things you can hear from your desk in your class when you are having a test.

3. Imagine you are Ondieki. You are in the playground after the test. Oyoo has forgotten Questions Four and Five in the test, and also the answers to these questions. You tell him the questions and answers again. Write what you told Oyoo.

4. Imagine you are Mr Angwenyi. Say what you noticed about Mutyaba, Ondieki and Oyoo during the test, and say what you think about their results.

14

Before you begin reading

Study these words and expressions:

conductor: the person who sells tickets on a bus

> *I saw that the* **conductor** *was wearing a leather bag, into which he put my money.*

cyclist: someone riding a bicycle

> *When* **cyclists** *hear a car behind them, they often ride off the tarmac on to the earth at the side of the road.*

all at once: suddenly

> *I had just gone to bed, when* **all at once** *there was a knock at the door.*

Reading passage

At last the bus appeared round a bend. Anok left the shade of the tree and walked to the edge of the road. For a moment he was afraid that the driver would not see him. But when two young women joined him at the roadside, he heard the engine slow down, and he knew ₅ it would be all right.

When he had climbed up into the bus, someone shouted his name. He looked forward and saw Drani waving his hand to tell him to come and join him. Anok pushed his way past some standing passengers ₁₀ and sat down beside his friend on the edge of the seat, just as the bus began to move. 'I did not think you would be on this bus,' said Anok. 'Are you going into Gulu?'

'That's right,' answered Drani.

15 'But our school doesn't open again for two weeks,' Anok said. 'That's your school box under your feet, isn't it?'

'Yes,' said Drani. 'I'm going to spend the rest of the holidays with an uncle of mine who lives in Gulu.
20 I can walk to the school from his house.'

The boys had talked for about ten minutes, when Anok was suddenly thrown forwards against another passenger, and fell to the floor. The bus seemed to jump madly up and down, and then boxes, bags, and bodies
25 dropped heavily on to him. All at once everything stopped moving, and the air was full of shouts and screams:

'I'm dying! Oh! Help! Give me air! My leg, oh! I'm dead! Let me get out!'

30 Anok fought his way out of the things that had fallen on him. He found he was standing on the side of one of the seats, and his head was out of a window. He understood at once what had happened and climbed out. Three men were already running away from the
35 bus. Anok nearly followed, but a shout from inside made him turn and help his friend to get free.

The two boys, the driver and the conductor pulled eleven more passengers out of the bus. They had to leave one old woman inside because she screamed
40 when they tried to move her. Nobody else seemed to be badly hurt. Some passengers were so frightened that they could only sit on the grass. The others went to the other side of the bus, where bicycles, baskets and fruit

16

lay all over the ground. While they were gathering their things, they talked angrily, saying that the driver had been very careless.

While Drani was getting his box from inside the bus, Anok walked up to the road, where several cyclists, two cars and a lorry had already stopped. He saw the deep marks made in the thick dust by the wheels of the bus. He noticed, too, that the road curved sharply as it went down the steep slope into the valley. Anok did not think it was all the fault of the driver. When Drani came and told him that one of the front tyres was punctured, Anok was sure the passengers were wrong to feel angry.

Test your understanding

1. When Anok heard the engine slow down,
   A. he knew that the driver would stop.
   B. he knew that the driver had seen him.
   C. he was happy because he would soon meet Drani.
   D. he left the shade of the tree.

2. When Anok saw Drani on the bus, he thought Drani was
   A. on his way home.
   B. on his way back to school.
   C. going to visit his uncle.
   D. going to walk to school.

3. When the bus stopped, it was
   A. upside-down on the road.
   B. lying on its side across the road.

C. lying on its side away from the road.

D. on its wheels but off the road.

4. The number of passengers in the bus was
   A. twenty.
   B. twelve.
   C. seventeen.
   D. fourteen.

5. Anok became sure that it was not the driver's fault at all
   A. when he saw the deep marks in the thick dust.
   B. because he noticed the bend in the road and the steep slope.
   C. because Drani came and told him.
   D. when he learnt that there had been a puncture.

Answer questions in writing

1. You were standing near the bus stop from the time the bus appeared until Anok climbed in. Write down what happened, in the right order.

2. Say what you think happened to the bus from the time when Anok fell to the floor until everything stopped moving.

3. How did the passengers feel after being pulled out of the bus?

4. The bus was carrying some passengers. What else was it carrying?

5. Several things had made it difficult for the driver to keep the bus on the road. One other thing had made it impossible for him. What were these things?

Imagine and write

1. Imagine you are the driver of the bus. Another bus has stopped on the road and you are explaining to the driver of that bus how it all happened. Write what you tell him.

2. Imagine you are Drani and write about what you did, saw, heard and felt from the time you saw Anok getting on the bus until he pulled you out.

3. Some passengers became angry because they thought the driver had been careless. Imagine you are one of them. Say what you think of the driver and tell about the difficulties you are in.

4. Imagine you are Anok. You are talking to one of the passengers who has been angry. You show him that it was not the driver's fault after all. Write what you say to him.

5. A medical assistant has been called to look after the old woman in the bus. When he comes, what do you think he will do?

3   THE BALL GAME

Before you begin reading

Study these words:

to bounce: to rise into the air again after hitting the ground

> *Rubber balls* **bounce** *well on hard, dry ground, but not on soft, wet earth.*

to chase: to run after a person or a thing in order to catch him or it

The policeman **chased** *the thief.*

to aim: to point something in a direction before throwing it or shooting

The hunter **aimed** *his spear at the antelope and threw it with all his strength.*

The score was equal: Both teams had scored the same number of points or goals

When the whistle blew at the end of the game, **the score was equal** *and so the result of the match was a draw.*

Reading passage

'Here, Henry, catch!' shouted David.

He threw the ball high into the air, just as Joseph ran up to him. Joseph jumped, but the ball passed between his arms. It bounced once on the earth of the
5 playground, and Henry caught it as it rose.

Philip and Michael then ran towards Henry. He laughed and ran away, holding the ball in his right hand. They both chased him, but Henry was faster. He reached the tall tree and touched it with the ball.

10 'That's one point for us,' yelled David, and all his team cheered.

Henry threw the ball across to John. John walked to the main classroom building, touched the wall with the ball and threw it out to Michael. The game had started
15 again.

David's team then tried to get the ball back. Joseph caught Michael's throw and was running quickly through the middle of the playground when suddenly he slipped and the ball rolled out of his hand. William ran past him, picked up the ball and began to run back towards the tall tree. But Philip chased him and touched him, so he had to stop and throw the ball to someone else. He tried to throw it to one of his own team, but Michael caught it and ran and touched the short tree with it.

The score was now equal. The ball was thrown back to David who had run to the classroom building to start the game again, as he was the leader. He saw Samuel standing at the other side of the playground and aimed it at him. But he had aimed badly. The ball went in a different direction. It bounced twice and was caught by James, who quietly put it in his pocket.

There was an angry yell, and the two teams ran up. But James went on talking to other big boys as if nothing had happened.

'Give us back our ball,' said John.

James turned and looked at him. 'It went into those bushes,' he said.

'It didn't. It's in your pocket,' said two or three of the smaller boys.

'Run away,' said James. 'We're talking.'

David and Henry jumped forward and took hold of James's hands, while John tried to get his hand in James's pocket. But two bigger boys began to pull them away. Then the other five smaller boys joined in the fighting.

Suddenly the bell rang. The fight stopped and the boys ran across the playground. Half-way over, James pulled out the ball. He dropped it on the ground, and Joseph ran to pick it up and put it in his pocket.

Test your understanding

1. David was the leader of one team. The other leader was
   A. Henry.
   B. John.
   C. Joseph.
   D. Philip.

2. The exact number of boys in each team was
   A. four.
   B. five.
   C. eight.
   D. several.

3. The points were scored by
   A. David and John.
   B. Henry and William.
   C. Michael and David.
   D. Henry and Michael.

4. When James said that the ball had gone in the bushes,
   A. John tried to get the ball out of his pocket.
   B. a fight began at once.
   C. he was told it was in his pocket.
   D. David and Henry jumped forward.

5. The fight stopped
   A. when the smaller boys won.
   B. because it was the end of the break.
   C. as soon as Joseph picked up the ball.
   D. because the ball dropped out of James's pocket.

Answer questions in writing

1. David was the leader of one team. Write down the name of the other leader and say how you know who it was.

2. Write down the names of the boys in each team, starting with the leader.

3. Explain the way the game is played.

4. Write down the order in which the boys touched the ball after the first point had been scored, starting with John, until the ball touched the short tree.

5. Write down everything that James did with the ball.

Imagine and write

1. Imagine you are Henry. Say how you scored the first point.

2. Imagine you are John. Write out what you saw and did from the time when David tried to throw the ball towards Samuel until the bell rang.

3. Imagine you are James. Say why you took the ball from the smaller boys and tell about what happened after you had taken it.

4. Write about a game you like playing during break at school. Explain how you play it.

4 LENYA AND THE THIEF

Before you begin reading

Study these words and expressions:

to rinse: to wash soapy water out of clothes

> *Joan always **rinses** her clothes well before she hangs them up to dry.*

The sun is in my eyes: I am looking towards the sun, and it is so bright that I cannot see things clearly

> *We tried to see the aeroplane, but **the sun was in our eyes.***

to wheel a bicycle: to push a bicycle along and walk beside it

> *If there is a big, heavy load on your bicycle it is easier to **wheel it** than to ride it.*

dressed in white: wearing white clothes

> *The Sisters at the Catholic Hospital are always **dressed in white.***

Reading passage

Lenya was down at the river, washing one of his white shirts. He rubbed it well in the soapy water in his bucket, rinsed it in the river and spread it out on the grass to dry.

5   He had finished the shirts, and two pairs of shorts

were drying on a bush, when a voice shouted a greeting from the bridge.

'Good morning!'

Lenya looked up but the sun was in his eyes.

'Good morning,' he replied, still trying to see who it 10 was.

The man wheeled his bicycle over the bridge and down the steep path until he was standing beside Lenya.

'You started early,' said the man, with a smile.

'Yes,' replied Lenya looking carefully at the man, 15 who was wearing an old khaki shirt and trousers. Lenya had never seen him before.

Both of them heard a bicycle sliding to a stop in the sandy road.

'Hallo, Lenya!' The voice was Kyagunya's. 'A 20 visitor is at your home and wants to see you at once. He can't wait long.'

'Who is it?'

'I haven't seen him. I met your sister and she asked me to tell you.' 25

'Well, come down and look after my things, will you?'

'All right.'

Half an hour later Lenya returned to the river. But Kyagunya was not there. The other man had gone too. 30 His clothes were still there on the grass and bushes. No, one shirt was missing; two blue shirts were left but only one white. A pair of shorts had also disappeared.

Lenya ran down to the river. He could not understand why Kyagunya had gone away. Just then he saw the 35 pedal of a bicycle shining in the sun. The bicycle had been thrown behind a bush. It was the man's bicycle.

Lenya suddenly turned. Something or someone had moved under the bridge. He saw a hand come up
40 behind a rock, then a face—it was Kyagunya.

Lenya ran to him. Kyagunya's head was cut and bleeding. Lenya splashed water over his friend.

'That man——' Kyagunya said weakly.

'Yes, yes, I understand,' Lenya answered quickly.

45 After a minute Kyagunya felt stronger. With Lenya's help, he climbed up to the main road and sat on a rock, while his friend gathered up his things and tied them on the back of the man's bicycle.

When Lenya got up to the road again, pushing the
50 bicycle, he saw that the chain was broken. So he changed his plan, and made Kyagunya sit on the bicycle while he wheeled it along the road towards the hospital.

They had not gone far when a lot of people came towards them. In the middle was a policeman, holding
55 a man dressed in white. It was the thief. A schoolboy at the shops had seen the man on Kyagunya's bicycle and because of this he had been arrested. Then Lenya remembered that the visitor at his home had spoken of a robbery at Mpalo before he had told them that a new
60 secondary school would soon be opened at Biharamulo.

Test your understanding

1. Lenya could not see the man's face at first
   A. because the man had his back to the sun.
   B. because the bridge was too high.
   C. because the man was too far away.
   D. as the man was hidden by the bridge.

26

2. When Kyagunya came, Lenya had washed
   A. four shirts and nothing else.
   B. fewer shirts than pairs of shorts.
   C. two white shirts, two blue shirts and two pairs of khaki shorts.
   D. four shirts and at least two pairs of shorts.

3. After Lenya had gone to meet the visitor
   A. Kyagunya stayed on his bicycle up on the road.
   B. Kyagunya was struck down by the man.
   C. Kyagunya lent the man his bicycle.
   D. Kyagunya was washing a dirty shirt for Lenya when the man hit him over the head.

4. The man left his bicycle behind
   A. because he thought Kyagunya might need it.
   B. because Kyagunya's had a better strap.
   C. because its pedals would not make the back wheel turn.
   D. to make people think he had run away.

5. After climbing up the path to the bridge, the man
   A. rode away but was arrested for the Mpalo robbery.
   B. was stopped by a policeman for stealing Lenya's clothes.
   C. rode off in the direction of the hospital.
   D. tried to get to Biharamulo.

Answer questions in writing

1. Describe the clothes that Lenya had already washed when the man greeted him from the bridge.
2. Why was Lenya unable to decide whether he knew the man until he had come down the path?

3. What did Lenya's sister do after the visitor had told her he wanted to speak to Lenya?

4. What were the things which Lenya found difficult to understand when he returned to the river?

5. Why did the man take Lenya's clothes?

6. What things did Lenya strap on the back of the man's bicycle before helping Kyagunya to the hospital?

Imagine and write

1. Imagine you are Lenya. Say what you did during the half-hour in which you were away from the river.

2. Tell the story of what happened at the river during the half-hour when Lenya was away.

3. Imagine that you were the person at the shops who saw Kyagunya's bicycle. Write about how you noticed it, what you said and did, and how the man was arrested.

4. Imagine you are the man, and that you are before the judge. You took a small part in the Mpalo robbery, but then you were frightened and ran away. Write down what you tell the judge about what you did from the time when you ran away, until you got on Kyagunya's bicycle. Try to make the judge believe that you are not a very bad man.

5. Imagine you are Kyagunya. You are at the hospital, and you tell a person in the next bed how you were brought from under the bridge to the doctor's room. Write what you told him.

Before you begin reading

Study these words and expressions:

path: a narrow way to walk along

> *That* **path** *leads through the trees and down to the main road.*

to make my way: to go round or over things that are in my way

> *I* **made my way** *up the hill, which was covered with rocks and fallen trees.*

to take a deep breath: to fill your chest with air

> *Before you begin singing, you should* **take a deep breath.**

Reading passage

Mary was sitting in the shade of her mother's hut late one afternoon, when she heard a weak cry coming from the forest. She stood up at once, not knowing what it could be. The cry came again. Mary called for her mother, and then remembered that she had gone to get 5 water. Hearing the cry once more, Mary walked across to the edge of the forest and stood there.

Which path should she take? One went up towards the road that led to the church. She knew that path well, because she used it every Sunday. But the cry, 10 which she now heard again, did not seem to be coming

from up the hill. Another path led down towards the river. If she went down there, she would meet her mother on her way back. But she did not think the
15 cry had come from that direction. There was a third path between the other two, but very few people used it. Once her brother had come back from school along that path and had been punished by her father.

But when the cry came once more, she was sure that
20 this path was the right one for her to take. Although she was afraid, she set out along it, and was soon inside the dark forest. A monkey suddenly screamed high up in a tall grey tree, and Mary's heart beat faster, but she walked on. She had to make her way past bushes and
25 elephant grass that had grown across the path, and after a short time she could not see the path in front of her any more.

Just then she heard the cry again, very near her. She noticed something moving behind the bushes on
30 her right. She nearly ran away but then she saw that it was a goat. A second later its head appeared and, by the mark on its forehead, she knew it was her mother's.

Mary ran up and found that the goat had got its rope caught on the roots of a tree. By going round and
35 round the tree, it had made a big knot in the rope, which Mary took a long time to untie, because the goat kept on trying to get away.

At last she was able to free the rope from the tree. She held it tightly in one hand and stood up. But she
40 could not see where the path was. She tried several times to find it but each time thick grass and bushes stopped her. Then the goat found some leaves it liked and Mary was not strong enough to pull the animal

away. The daylight was getting weaker. Mary felt very
afraid. 45

Suddenly she heard her mother's voice calling her.
Mary took a deep breath and shouted back, telling her
mother that she was in the forest with the goat. Soon
Mary saw her mother appear and ran forward to meet
her. As they were walking home together with the 50
goat, Mary asked:

'Will Father punish me because I walked along this
path?'

'No,' replied her mother. 'You did it to save my
goat.' 55

But Mary knew that what her mother said was not
exactly true.

Test your understanding

1. Mary stood for a time at the edge of the forest
   A. because she knew her mother would soon be
      back.
   B. to decide which way to go.
   C. because thick grass and bushes stopped her from
      walking any further.
   D. because she was sure her father would punish
      her if she went into the forest.

2. Mary was afraid of setting out along the middle path
   A. when she heard the monkey scream.
   B. because nobody ever used it.
   C. because it was not often used and her father
      might be angry if she went on it.
   D. as the sun had already set.

3. The goat
   A. was held to the roots of a tree by its rope.
   B. was caught on some bushes.
   C. stood quite still while Mary untied the rope.
   D. was walking round and round the tree when Mary first saw it.

4. After untying the rope, Mary was unable to take the goat home
   A. because it was too dark.
   B. and so she let it find some leaves to eat while she waited.
   C. because she was too afraid.
   D. as she had lost the way.

5. Mary had gone into the forest
   A. to save her mother's goat.
   B. to find out where the middle path went.
   C. to find out what was making the cry.
   D. to meet her mother.

Answer questions in writing

1. How many times did Mary hear the cry before she set out into the forest?

2. Why did Mary think that the middle path was the right one for her to take?

3. In order to get the goat away from the tree, what exactly did Mary have to do?

4. After Mary had untied the rope, what reasons did she have for feeling afraid until her mother came?

5. What was not exactly true in the words used by Mary's mother?

Imagine and write

1. Imagine you are Mary's mother and say what you did, saw, heard and felt from the time you left Mary at your hut, until you found her again.

2. The goat should not have been so far away in the forest. It had been tied to a stick near the back of the hut earlier that day. Tell the story of how it got free, went into the forest, and got its rope caught.

3. Mary's brother was punished once when he used the middle path. Imagine that Mary's father is telling her what dangers there are in the forest and why he punished his son at that time. Write down what he said.

4. The following day, when Mary returned from school, the goat was missing again. Mary saw from the marks on the ground that it had gone into the forest once more. Write about how Mary went into the forest, found it and brought it back.

6   THE HOSPITAL VISIT

Before you begin reading

Study these words and expressions:

ward: a large room in a hospital where people sleep

> *In one corner of the* **ward** *there was a man with a broken leg.*

thermometer: a glass stick used to find out how hot a person is, especially when he is ill

The nurse told me to open my mouth, and put one end of the **thermometer** *under my tongue.*

to take his pulse: to see how fast a man's heart is beating by holding his wrist and counting the beats

Every morning the nurse came **to take his pulse.**

Reading passage

When we got off the bus, I saw in front of me three tall, grey buildings. Each of them had more windows than I could count, and a lot of yellow flowers were growing around them. While my father was asking the
5 way, I looked at the people walking past us. Most of the women were wearing bright red, purple or green cotton dresses. Some of the dresses reached down to the ankle, but usually they stopped at the knee.

'It's the building on the right,' said my father. 'He's
10 in Ward 3.'

We all began to follow him along the path. My mother had to walk slowly because of Peter and Janet, but John and I ran past Father to the door.

At last we stood outside Ward 3. The doors were
15 open, and inside we could see a very long room with a lot of beds in it. There seemed to be someone in every bed. Many of the people in the beds were looking at the doorway. I was glad I had put on my new yellow dress.

34

'There he is,' said Mother, pushing me as she walked through with the baby. 20

I took Peter's hand and we walked down the room. We stopped at a bed with 18 painted in black on the wall behind it. At first I could see nothing but blankets and bandages. Then I noticed some fingers, but I couldn't see the rest of the hand or the arm. My mother seemed 25 to be talking to some bandages at the other end of the bed, so I knew that those bandages must be around Charles's head. But I did not really believe it was my brother inside the bandages until I walked to the other end of the bed and saw his nose, mouth and chin 30 and one eye. The rest of his head was covered with bandages. He looked at me and said in a weak voice:

'Hallo, Mary.'

'What is your other eye doing?' I asked.

'It's shut,' he answered, but he seemed to smile. 35

After talking for a few minutes with Charles, Mother went away to cook some food for him, and the three younger children went to watch her. I sat on the empty bed near my elder brother.

'Can my bicycle be mended?' Charles asked. 40

'No,' Father replied. 'The car ran right over it. We must thank God that it did not run over you. When it hit your bicycle you were thrown into the air.'

'But I don't remember anything,' said Charles.

'Yes, I know. You told me yesterday,' answered 45 Father. 'You had no time to understand what was happening before you hit that rock.'

'I shall put a red light on the back of my next bicycle,' said Charles. 'Then perhaps it will not happen again.'

'It's time to go,' said a voice behind us. I turned 50

35

to see a nurse standing there in a beautiful white dress with silver buttons and a little green cap. 'You must not make him tired,' she added.

I stood up, and she smiled at me.

55 'How badly is my brother hurt?' I asked.

'There's nothing more than you can see now,' she said. 'He's lucky. If he does what he is told he should be home in three or four weeks.'

I watched while the nurse put a thermometer in 60 Charles's mouth and held his wrist to take his pulse. She was looking at a small gold wristwatch. When she had finished, Charles had shut his eye and seemed to be sleeping.

Test your understanding

1. Most of the women near the hospital buildings
   A. were wearing bright red cotton dresses.
   B. had put on dresses that reached to the knee.
   C. were wearing very long red, purple or green cotton dresses.
   D. had put on dresses of every colour you can imagine.

2. There were five children in the family. John was
   A. the eldest.
   B. younger than Peter.
   C. the third child.
   D. older than Mary.

3. Mary asked Charles what his other eye was doing
   A. as it was too dark in the room for her to see clearly.

B. because she could not understand why it was shut.

C. when he seemed to smile.

D. since it was covered in bandages.

4. Charles had been hurt
   A. when he was walking across the road.
   B. while he was cycling one day.
   C. at night when he was riding his bicycle.
   D. when a car crashed into the front of his bicycle.

5. When Mary went into the ward
   A. a lot of the people in bed were looking towards her.
   B. everyone was looking at her new yellow dress.
   C. she saw that there was someone in every bed.
   D. she noticed Charles at once.

Answer questions in writing

1. Write down the names of the children, starting with the eldest and finishing with the youngest.

2. What parts of Charles's body were hurt?

3. What coloured things did Mary notice outside the hospital?

4. Had anybody in the family visited Charles before? Give a reason for your answer.

5. What coloured things did Mary notice inside the hospital?

Imagine and write

1. Imagine you are Charles. Say what happened and how you felt when your family came to visit you.

2. Imagine you are Mary's mother. Say what you did, saw, heard and felt when you visited the hospital.

3. Imagine you are the nurse. Say what you saw and did from the time when you came into the ward to speak to Charles's visitors until the family left the ward.

4. You know that Mary was wearing a new yellow dress. Say how you think the other persons in the family were dressed.

7   THE STORM

Reading passage

When the bell rang for afternoon school, there were
heavy rainclouds in the sky, and a strong, cold wind
began to blow. Catherine was glad to get inside the
classroom, where it was still quite warm. She saw
Josephine and Hilda shutting the windows.   5

Five minutes later the teacher had to stop talking
about soil erosion. The rain was beating so loudly on
the corrugated iron roof that Catherine could not even
hear what Hilda was trying to tell her. The thunder
was rumbling all the time, too, and often broke out in 10
roars and crashes. It was so dark that the girls sitting
in one corner of the room could not read their books,
as Miss Bagutanya had told them. To give Rosemary
something else to do, the teacher asked her to go and
get some buckets to catch the water that would soon 15
come through the roof.

A big drop of water fell suddenly on Catherine's
book, just on the spot where she was reading. She was
so surprised that several more drops had fallen there
before she pulled her book away. Soon there was a 20
small pool of water on her desk, and she moved along
the bench nearer to Hilda. Then the drops began to
follow each other quickly and splash water all round
when they struck the pool on the desk.

Hilda, Catherine, and a girl sitting in front stood up 25

to move further away. Just then the door opened and Rosemary walked in. One bucket was put in each of the usual places, near the door, near the blackboard and in the middle of the room. Catherine and Hilda 30 hoped they would get the only bucket left.

All at once there was a crash and the sound of tearing metal. Wind and rain were sweeping into one corner of the room. Miss Bagutanya looked quickly at the roof and shouted:

35 'Outside!'

The girls rushed to the door and squeezed through. As Catherine left, she heard Miss Bagutanya slam the door shut behind her and shout:

'Go to the staff room!'

40 Rosemary led the way, running through the rain and holding a bucket upside-down over her head. The other girls followed her across the slippery earth of the compound. Catherine had to jump across a small stream that was carrying brown water down the slope away 45 from the school.

'There,' said Miss Bagutanya in Catherine's ear, when they reached the other side. 'The storm will soon be over. You've had a lesson in soil erosion after all.'

Test your understanding

1. Catherine's seat was
   A. in the middle of the room.
   B. near the teacher.
   C. in the darkest corner of the room.
   D. near Hilda.

2. Miss Bagutanya stopped teaching
   A. because water was dropping in through the roof.
   B. as the girls could not hear her.
   C. until Rosemary returned.
   D. when wind and rain swept into the room.

3. The teacher asked Rosemary to get some buckets
   A. because this was Rosemary's usual job.
   B. to catch the water that was coming in.
   C. because Rosemary had nothing to do.
   D. since Rosemary had finished her book.

4. Catherine was surprised
   A. that several more drops had fallen on her book.
   B. when she saw a pool of water on her desk.
   C. when a drop of water fell on her book, because water had never come through there before.
   D. when a big drop of water fell on her.

5. What happened to the buckets?
   A. Three were put in the usual places, and one was given to Catherine.
   B. Two were put in the usual places and one near the blackboard.
   C. The girls used them to keep the rain off their heads.
   D. Three were put in the usual places and Rosemary kept the fourth.

6. When wind and rain swept into the room, Miss Bagutanya
   A. looked quickly at the roof and shouted: 'Go outside!'
   B. was afraid that the whole roof might be blown away.

C. told the girls to leave because she wanted them to learn about soil erosion outside.

D. could not decide what to do.

7. When they all left the classroom,
   A. Miss Bagutanya came out last.
   B. Catherine and Rosemary were together.
   C. Miss Bagutanya was pushing Catherine from behind.
   D. the girls went through the door in good order.

Answer questions in writing

1. Why did Miss Bagutanya say: 'You've had a lesson in soil erosion after all'?

2. Where was Rosemary's seat? Give a reason for your answer.

3. Why did wind and rain suddenly sweep into the classroom?

4. What changes had the storm made to the compound?

5. Write five sentences about sounds that the girls heard during the storm.

Imagine and write

1. Imagine that you are Rosemary and write about what you saw, heard and did that afternoon.

2. Imagine you are Miss Bagutanya. You are in the headmistress's office, giving her a report of what has happened. She wants to write a letter to the managers about it. Write out what you said to her.

3. Imagine you are Miss Bagutanya. The storm is over

and afternoon school is finished. You are in the staff room with your best friend, who is also a teacher, and you are telling her what happened and what you thought and felt. Write out what you told her.

4. Imagine you are Catherine and say what you saw Miss Bagutanya do and heard her say that afternoon.

5. Write eight sentences about things you see, hear and do when it rains heavily at your school.

8   THE DISPENSARY

Before you begin reading

Study these words:

dispensary: a building where medicines are given out and where doctors sometimes see people who are ill

The nearest **dispensary** *was eight miles away from our village.*

sling: a piece of cloth fastened at the ends so as to make a bag in the middle to carry things in

In some parts of Africa, babies are carried in **slings** *on their mothers' backs.*

itchy: sore in a way which makes you want to scratch

A mosquito bite is **itchy.**

medicine: something to cure an illness, usually to be swallowed

The nurse told me to take two large spoonfuls of green **medicine** *twice a day.*

43

gently: softly and slowly, so as not to break or hurt or surprise

She took hold of the glass **gently** *and put it in the cupboard.*

Reading passage

Although it was early, the benches in the waiting room were already full, and other people were also standing near the dispensary doors. Mrs Lubwama found a place to sit in the shade of a wall outside. She put down
5 her bag, bent forward a little and untied the knot holding the sling. Taking her baby by one arm, she put him on her hip and pulled off the piece of cloth she had carried him in. Then she sat down in the shade, folded the cloth to make a small mat, and laid the baby on it.
10 From her place, Mrs Lubwama could see inside the waiting-room. Near the door an old man with white hair was sitting. He was dressed in torn, dirty clothes, his feet were badly swollen and he looked very tired. Next to him were two women with small children.
15 She noticed that one of the children was coughing a lot. Further along the same bench was a schoolgirl, and next to her the old woman who sold fish at the market. On the opposite bench she saw a small child who kept scratching his leg. When the child's mother got up to go
20 in to the doctor, Mrs Lubwama noticed the itchy place behind the knee. Just then she heard someone greet her.

'Good morning, Margaret.' It was Mrs Kaddu.

'Good morning, Ruth,' answered Mrs Lubwama with a smile, as her friend sat down beside her.

Mrs Lubwama showed the baby's back to her friend. 'But I've just seen another child with the same sort of thing, so perhaps it's not my fault.'

'I'm sure it's not,' said Mrs Kaddu. 'Poor little boy! Does he sleep all right at night?'   30

'Not very well, I'm afraid,' answered Mrs Lubwama. 'I have to take him up two or three times and wash the skin with a wet cloth to take away the itch. Then he falls asleep again for a few hours.'

The two women rested and talked for an hour or two. 35 Then they moved to a seat inside the waiting-room, which had become half empty. It was not long before Mrs Lubwama was called in to see the doctor.

'Yes,' he said, touching the baby's back gently with his finger. 'That must be quite painful. What have you 40 done to try to cure it?'

When Mrs Lubwama told him, he was a little angry. He ordered her to stop at once, and instead to spread on the baby's back something soft and white, which he showed her in a silver tin. While he wrote something 45 quickly on a piece of paper, Mrs Lubwama looked around his room at the bottles in an open cupboard and at the long, high bed against the wall. On her way out, Mrs Lubwama gave in the piece of paper and got a small, round tin.   50

That afternoon she began doing what the doctor had said and three days later she was able to sleep right through the night without having to wake up.

Test your understanding

1. When Mrs Lubwama reached the hospital,
   A. she sat down in the waiting room.
   B. she was too late to find a seat on the benches.
   C. she went to stand with the people near the hospital door.
   D. she laid the baby on the cloth and sat down.

2. Inside the waiting room,
   A. the schoolgirl sat opposite the small child with an itch behind the knee.
   B. Mrs Lubwama could see only one old person.
   C. the schoolgirl was sitting beside the man with swollen feet.
   D. nobody was sitting beside the mother of the child with itchy skin.

3. At the dispensary, Mrs Lubwama thought it was perhaps not her fault
   A. that another child had the same sort of thing.
   B. that her baby had a sore back.
   C. because her child was ill too.
   D. because she had just seen another child.

4. Before the visit to the dispensary, Mrs Lubwama's baby
   A. never woke her up at night-time.
   B. had to be washed very often during the night.
   C. had to be washed during the night because it was dirty.
   D. needed more attention than it had needed before.

5. The doctor was a little angry
   A. because a wet cloth would not cure an itchy skin.
   B. when he heard that the baby woke up at night.

C. because he had never seen skin like this before.

D. as he had hurt his finger on the baby's back.

Answer questions in writing

1. When Mrs Lubwama set off for hospital that morning, she put the baby in a sling on her back. Explain exactly how she did this.

2. How many people did Mrs Lubwama notice before Mrs Kaddu greeted her? How many of them were boys as far as you know?

3. What had Mrs Lubwama thought about the itch on her own child's back before she saw the itchy skin behind the other child's knee?

4. Before Mrs Lubwama visited the dispensary, how did she know when to wash the baby's skin at night?

5. What did the doctor tell Mrs Lubwama not to do? What showed her that she had got the right thing for her baby from the hospital?

Imagine and write

1. Imagine you are the doctor. After all the people have gone, you are talking with the nurse about the morning's work. You tell her about Mrs Lubwama and her baby. Write what you said.

2. Imagine you are Mrs Kaddu. You are in the room with the doctor. Explain what is wrong with you.

3. Imagine you are the schoolgirl. You noticed some of the things that Mrs Lubwama saw, and others that she did not see. Write about what you saw and heard in the waiting-room.

4. Imagine you are Mrs Lubwama. Mrs Kaddu comes to visit you when your baby is well and happy again. You tell her about how the baby got better. Write what you said.

9   THE SOLDIER

Before you begin reading

Study these words:

shopkeeper: a person who owns a small shop and sells things in it

    *Mr Musazi became a **shopkeeper** after retiring from his work on the railways.*

counter: the table between the shopkeeper and those who come to buy

    *I put my bag on the **counter** and took out two empty bottles.*

rags: torn pieces of cloth or torn clothes

    *Very poor people are often dressed in **rags**.*

Swahili: a language spoken in some parts of Eastern Africa

    *He speaks **Swahili** so fast that I cannot understand him.*

fist: the hand, with fingers and thumb tightly shut

    *The two schoolboys began hitting each other with their **fists**.*

Reading passage

'A small packet of tea, please,' I said. It was hot inside the shop and the air did not move.

The shopkeeper turned around again and put his hand into a cupboard. Suddenly a yellow and red packet was on the counter between us. I saw that he 5 was looking over my head, waiting.

'A packet of Crown Bird. That's all we need today, thank you.'

'Two shillings and ninety cents,' said the shopkeeper, placing the cigarettes beside the other things. I was 10 sure he did not like children.

As I gave him the money, I noticed that he was smiling. I looked quickly down at my dress to see if I had buttoned it wrongly. Then a man near me laughed and said: 15

'There's the soldier again.'

Everyone in the shop looked out towards the main road. Not very far away a man was walking down the middle of the tarmac, along the broken white line. He was dressed in khaki rags and carried a thick stick 20 against his left shoulder. He kept on shouting in Swahili as he marched along.

'The rainy season must be near,' a woman behind me said.

'Yes, he comes every year at this time,' added 25 another.

'Nobody knows where he goes when the rainy season is over,' said a teacher from my school.

'But he speaks Swahili,' I said. Everyone in the shop laughed. 30

49

'I speak Swahili,' said the teacher. 'But that man only knows a few words that he learnt when he was a soldier.'

During this time the soldier had marched much 35 nearer. I could not tell what part of the country he was born in, for his hair was very long and thick and his face very thin. I did not know how he found food to eat, but I thought that perhaps he stole it. His wild eyes frightened me.

40 Just then I heard a car coming down the hill. I saw that the soldier had not heard it. Its engine became louder as it went faster and faster. I ran out of the shop without knowing why, and then stopped. I had noticed that the soldier was looking at me. He took a 45 step towards me, the brakes of the car screamed and a big black shape shot past between him and me. As it raced away and got back on the tarmac, the soldier shouted after it in a language I had never heard before and shook his fist. Then he put his stick on his shoulder 50 again, turned away and marched on up the hill, still in the middle of the road, and shouting in Swahili at the top of his voice.

When I got home, I gave my mother the things I had bought. As she was pouring the sugar into a tin, 55 I told her about the soldier.

'Is he still alive?' asked my mother in surprise. 'He used to march along like that when we lived here before.'

That night I dreamt that the soldier was walking 60 towards me. He was talking to someone in my own language, when a big black lorry ran over him and killed him. Six weeks later I heard at school that the mad soldier had been found dead on the road near Bugiri.

Test your understanding

1. In the shop, the girl
   A. bought at least three things.
   B. paid two shillings and ninety cents for the tea and cigarettes.
   C. liked talking with the shopkeeper.
   D. buttoned up her dress correctly.

2. When the girl first saw the soldier,
   A. he was marching along beside the road.
   B. he was wearing torn clothes.
   C. he was walking away from the shop.
   D. he was shouting in a language that the girl had never heard before.

3. The soldier
   A. often came just before the rainy season began.
   B. always stayed in the district during the rainy season.
   C. usually left the district during the rainy season.
   D. spoke Swahili well.

4. The big black car did not kill the soldier
   A. because the girl screamed.
   B. since the soldier had stepped out of the way.
   C. as it was going too fast.
   D. because the driver braked and steered out of the way.

5. The soldier
   A. was killed by a lorry near Bugiri.

51

B. was run over by a big black lorry and died later near Bugiri.

C. had been seen before by the girl's mother.

D. could speak three languages.

Answer questions in writing

1. What had the girl's mother asked her to buy?

2. Describe the soldier.

3. How many languages are used or spoken about in the passage, and who can speak them?

4. What did the driver of the car do in order not to knock down the soldier?

5. What does the last paragraph of the passage tell you about the soldier?

Imagine and write

1. Imagine you are the shopkeeper. Say what you saw, heard and did from the time the girl entered your shop until you noticed the soldier.

2. Imagine that the soldier was killed by a taxi on the road, and that you are the taxi-driver. Say what happened.

3. Imagine that you are the teacher at the girl's school. The children in your class have all heard about the soldier and want you to tell them who he is and what he does. Write what you say to them.

4. You are a police officer at Bugiri. A brother of the dead man is in your office. He is explaining the reasons for the kind of life his brother had lived after he had stopped being a soldier. Write what he says.

Before you begin reading

Study these words:

to drain: to make water flow away from swamps or wet land

> *Before you can grow crops in a swamp, you must* **drain** *it.*

habit: something that a person usually does

> *The teacher had a* **habit** *of telling the class to sit up straight at the beginning of each lesson.*

Reading passage

From the rock he was sitting on, Baroraho could see across the deep valley towards the mountain. In the morning sunshine, the gullies high on the mountainside showed very clearly. Below them he could see the bright green plantations of banana in the village of 5 Rwakaimara. Far below him lay the thick papyrus swamps along the valley, with small green or yellow fields where parts of the swamps had been drained and crops had been sown.

He stretched. It was hot in the sun, but a strong 10 wind blew across the top of the hill and helped to make him feel cooler. Far off in the east he noticed small white clouds low down in the blue sky. Just then he heard a shout.

53

15 'Baroraho!'

He could just see that someone was coming through the tall grass up the steep slope towards him. The voice had seemed like his younger brother's, but he did not believe it could be. Rushambuza spent most of the 20 day playing with other boys, and was never to be seen when there was work to do. Suddenly he saw that he was wrong.

'Have you really come to look after the goats?' Baroraho asked a few minutes later.

25 'Of course,' replied Rushambuza. 'You can go down now.'

As Baroraho came near the back of the huts, he could hear his father talking with another man. The visitor was speaking in a rather quiet voice, but just then he 30 began to cough, and Baroraho understood at once why Rushambuza had come to look after the goats. The visitor was Uncle Tindyebwa.

Baroraho walked into the compound, where the two men were sitting on wooden chairs. He stopped in front 35 of his uncle and greeted him politely.

'Yes,' said Uncle Tindyebwa, after the greeting was over, 'that is how young men are nowadays. I was telling your father the sad news about Rukyalekere's eldest son.'

40 'Is he dead?' asked Baroraho quickly.

'It would perhaps be better if he was,' replied Uncle Tindyebwa. 'He is in prison.'

Baroraho wanted to ask why, but Uncle Tindyebwa was looking so sharply at him that he did not dare. 45 He wished he could run away as his brother had done. Then he would not have to listen to the speech about

54

the bad habits of young people that Uncle Tindyebwa always gave.

'Yes, in prison,' Uncle Tindyebwa went on, 'for three years. When he comes out, he will still not understand that he has done a bad thing. He will steal again. But when I was young, we knew how to punish thieves in a way they didn't forget.'

The old man smiled proudly, and leaned forwards on his big walking stick. Then the smile disappeared.

'But those days have gone. Now children are sent to school. Good schools give heavy punishments. That is why your father and I have decided that we shall send you to Rwentobo. The letter from the headmaster is in my pocket. It is all arranged. You begin next month.'

Test your understanding

1. The bananas were growing
   A. lower down the slope of the hill Baroraho was on.
   B. between the gullies on the mountain side.
   C. between the gullies and the bottom of the valley.
   D. in the small green and yellow fields.

2. Baroraho was sitting
   A. on a rock on a steep slope.
   B. in a hot, windless place.
   C. on a rock on the top of a hill.
   D. amongst the tall grass on the slope of a hill.

3. Rushambuza came to look after the goats
   A. so that his brother should have a rest.

B. because he did not like hearing what Uncle Tindyebwa said about young people.

C. as his father had told him to do so.

D. because it was near the end of the day and he had finished playing with other boys.

4. Baroraho understood that the visitor was Uncle Tindyebwa
   A. when he heard his father talking with another man.
   B. because his voice was rather quiet.
   C. from the way he coughed.
   D. because Rushambuza had come to look after the goats.

5. Uncle Tindyebwa
   A. did not think Rukyalekere's son would change his habits.
   B. thought that prison helped people to become better.
   C. did not agree with heavy punishments.
   D. was proud of his big walking stick.

Answer questions in writing

1. What was growing on the slopes on the two sides of the valley?

2. Why was Baroraho not sure who had called his name?

3. What sort of a person was Rushambuza?

4. What did Rushambuza not like about Uncle Tindyebwa?

5. What did Uncle Tindyebwa think about punishment?

6. If you walk from the top of the hill where Baroraho was sitting, cross the valley and climb the mountain, what will you pass through?

Imagine and write

1. Imagine you are Rushambuza. You had been playing with another boy and were coming home when you heard your father talking with the visitor. Say what you did and thought from that time until you were left alone on the hill.

2. Imagine you are Uncle Tindyebwa. Baroraho has not yet arrived. You are telling Baroraho's father what Rukyalekere's son did. Write what you say.

3. Imagine you are Baroraho. You are at Rwentobo school. Uncle Tindyebwa is paying part of your fees. You are telling a new friend about your uncle. Write what you tell him.

4. Imagine you are Baroraho. Your father is a kinder man than Uncle Tindyebwa. That evening you ask your father what he thinks about punishments. Write what he says to you.

11   CHARLES AND THE BICYCLE

Before you begin reading

Study these words:

hymn: song to be sung in church

We sang four **hymns** *in church last Sunday.*

congregation: the people who have come to attend church

Every Christmas there is a very large **congregation** *at our church.*

crowd: a large number of people together

A **crowd** *had gathered at the ferry and was waiting to cross.*

The **crowd** *roared when Nkalubo scored the winning goal.*

Reading passage

When Charles heard the signal, he stood up with everyone else in the church to sing the last hymn. The leader sang the first few words and then all the congregation joined in. Charles tried to hear the women's voices but
5 it was difficult, as many of the boys near him were singing loudly. He could tell that they would be glad to leave the church.

Charles was glad too. He had found the sermon very long and had only understood that it was about angels
10 and heaven. Perhaps his father would be able to explain more when they got outside. He looked through the open door at his new bicycle, which he had put against the wall and locked carefully. Some other bicycles were standing against his, but none of them were so clean
15 and bright.

When the music stopped, the boys pushed their way out of the door. Charles had to wait a little for other people to take their bicycles, before he got his. He unlocked it, wheeled it away from the wall and got on.

Then he cycled slowly through the crowd outside the church. It was so easy to ride this new bicycle. He had learnt on an old one, which shook and squeaked and had broken pedals.

Charles saw his father talking with some other men. He knew that he would have to wait for at least half an hour before they set off home.

'Hallo, Charles,' said Andrew, suddenly appearing beside Charles. 'Is that yours?'

'Yes,' Charles proudly replied, putting the brakes on and placing one foot on the ground.

'Does it work?' asked Andrew, touching the bell.

'Of course,' Charles answered, and rang it.

Andrew looked up at Charles. His eyes were shining with excitement. 'May I sit on your bicycle?'

As Andrew was his best friend, Charles agreed. 'You may even ride it over to the school and back, if you like,' he added.

Andrew was off at once. As soon as he had left the crowd behind he began to go faster and faster. Suddenly he saw that he was going straight towards a big heap of bricks in the school compound. He stopped pedalling and put the brakes on. The wheels slipped on the wet earth and he fell into some thick mud. He got up quickly, but his hands and legs were covered with mud. So were the bicycle wheels, one pedal, the bell and a corner of the seat.

Charles ran up and lifted his bicycle carefully out of the mud. It was Andrew's fault, and Charles was a bit angry.

'I'm very sorry,' said Andrew. 'I'll help you to clean it.'

59

'All right,' said Charles. 'I don't think you've broken or scratched anything.'

Using a piece of cloth and water from the tap behind the school, they washed the mud away. The bicycle soon glittered again in the sunlight, as bright and clean as it had been before.

Test your understanding

1. In the church
   A. the congregation sang the hymn from beginning to end.
   B. the women began singing at the same time as the men.
   C. all the boys near Charles were singing loudly.
   D. some of the boys near Charles were not singing.

2. Charles's bicycle
   A. was standing between two other older bicycles.
   B. was outside the church.
   C. was standing against the wall with one wheel inside the church.
   D. was cleaner and brighter than any other bicycle that Charles could see.

3. One of the reasons why Charles found it easier to ride his new bicycle than the old one was
   A. that it had pedals.
   B. that it squeaked more.
   C. that it worked better.
   D. that the ground was dry everywhere that Sunday morning.

4. When Andrew appeared beside him, Charles
   A. was riding slowly through the crowd.
   B. had put his foot on the ground.
   C. was ringing the bell on his bicycle.
   D. got off his bicycle at once.

5. Andrew put the brakes on
   A. when he saw the mud.
   B. because he was going faster and faster.
   C. when he saw the bricks ahead.
   D. in order to turn around.

Answer questions in writing

1. Charles was not the last person to come to church that morning. Can you show that this must be true?

2. Why was Charles happy when they were singing the hymn?

3. Why could Charles not take his bicycle as soon as he was outside the church?

4. Give all the reasons for Andrew's fall from the bicycle?

5. What did Charles do to his bicycle from the time when it fell into the mud, until the end of the story?

Imagine and write

1. Imagine that you are one of the boys who was at church. You were standing at the edge of the crowd when Andrew cycled past you. Say what you saw him do, and what you thought about it.

2. Imagine that you are Andrew. Say what you did to help Charles at the tap and how you tried to get yourself clean afterwards.

3. Write eight sentences about what you do, see and hear when you leave your church or mosque.

4. Imagine you are Charles. Andrew has gone home and you are standing near your father, who has nearly finished talking. You are telling your brother what happened when you lent your bicycle to Andrew. Write what you say.

5. Imagine that you have a new bicycle. Write eight sentences describing it and say what you feel about it.

12 TERESA CLEANS A ROOM

Before you begin reading

Study these words:

to scrub: to clean by brushing hard with soap and water

> *The hospital floor was washed every day and* **scrubbed** *once a week to keep it clean.*

recipe: an explanation of how to cook a special kind of food

> *Schoolgirls are sometimes given new* **recipes** *in their domestic science lessons.*

Reading passage

Teresa sat down on a stool to rest. She looked sadly
at the bucket in front of her, half full of dirty water.
She had begun at seven that morning, a few minutes
after her husband had left, to clean the back room in
their little house in the town. She could not understand 5
how the people who had lived there before had made
the back room so dirty. She had used plenty of soap, a
hard brush and a cloth and worked with all her strength.
But the room, which she had emptied completely before
she began working, did not seem to be any cleaner. 10

She got up, walked over to the window and looked
out. She could see that the soil in the garden was too
poor to grow good vegetables, and the whole garden was
far too small for a banana plantation. She began thinking
of her father's farm in the country, which she had left 15
only two weeks before to get married. That had been a
wonderful day!

Suddenly she noticed that the bus had stopped up
on the main road. It must be half-past eleven. Two
minutes later she was on her hands and knees again, 20
scrubbing hard with the brush and with clean, soapy
water.

All at once there was a knock at the door.

'Anybody at home?' a voice called out.

'Ursula!' Teresa shouted, running to the door to 25
make sure she was right. 'Come in, come in!'

She took Ursula by the hand and made her sit down
in the best chair in the front room.

'Was it difficult to find our house?' Teresa asked her
friend. 30

'Oh, no,' Ursula replied, smiling. 'I saw you at the tap outside while I was walking from the bus.'

For ten minutes they talked about their families and friends. Then Teresa looked sad.

35 'I didn't know it was such hard work to make a home,' she said, thinking of the back room. 'I thought it was quite easy in the country for my mother, but in these town houses the walls and floors seem to get so dirty. Come and see.'

40 'You must use a much stronger kind of soap,' said Ursula, after looking at the cleaning Teresa was doing. 'I'll write the name of the soap I use on this piece of paper. It smells nice too.'

'What can I do with that garden?' asked Teresa 45 unhappily.

Ursula laughed. 'Well, you can't grow much cotton or coffee, I agree. But you can grow quite a lot of vegetables, if you use manure.'

'I'll try that,' said Teresa. 'But the garden is very 50 small.'

Two hours later the two friends were still talking. Teresa had made some tea and put biscuits on a plate, and had spread a lovely blue cloth over the table near the best chair. Ursula had filled up a long sheet of 55 paper with the names of things to use, shops to visit and recipes to try out.

Suddenly she looked at her wristwatch. 'I must go,' she said, 'or I'll miss the bus home. My husband likes to have tea as soon as he comes back from work, and I 60 still have to cook the meat for tonight's meal.'

After Ursula had gone, Teresa bought some strong soap at the shop and began again. This time the dirt

disappeared quickly, and at the end of the day Teresa
proudly showed her husband the progress she had made.

'That's fine,' he said. 'I shall enjoy studying here.' 65

Test your understanding

1. While Teresa was sitting on the stool, she felt sad
   A. about the bucket in front of her.
   B. because her husband had left.
   C. when she saw she was making no progress.
   D. because she knew that the soap was not strong
      enough.

2. When she looked out over the garden, Teresa
   A. wished she had not married.
   B. wished that her husband was richer.
   C. thought happily of the day she was married.
   D. thought it was a wonderful day.

3. Teresa
   A. thought it was Ursula when she heard the voice
      at the door.
   B. knew it was Ursula at the door.
   C. had seen Ursula when she was getting water.
   D. had been seen by Ursula from the bus.

4. Ursula
   A. advised her friend to grow a little cotton or
      coffee.
   B. told Teresa to plant peas, beans and cabbages.
   C. explained to Teresa that she should add something
      to make the soil richer.
   D. agreed with her friend that the garden was
      useless.

5. Ursula left Teresa's house
   A. late in the morning.
   B. at exactly half-past one.
   C. at about three in the afternoon.
   D. about seven hours after Teresa's husband had left.

Answer questions in writing

1. What was in the back room when Teresa was cleaning it?
2. What did Teresa do in the two minutes after she saw the bus?
3. In what ways did Ursula help her friend during her visit?
4. What was the back room to be used for?
5. How did Teresa spend that day?

Imagine and write

1. Imagine you are Teresa. Say how you prepared to clean the back room, and what you did and thought during the morning before eleven o'clock.

2. Imagine that you are Teresa. It is three days after Ursula's visit. You have made a plan for growing vegetables in your garden, and you are explaining it to your husband. Write what you say to him.

3. Imagine you are Ursula. You have been married for three years, and you spent the first two of these years in the town where Teresa is now living. Explain what information you gave your friend on the long sheet of paper.

66

4. Imagine that you are Ursula. You visited Teresa again a year later. Write about the changes you saw in her house and garden.

13   THE COTTON HARVEST

Before you begin reading

Study these words and expressions:

tuft: the round white ball of cotton that breaks out of the pod

> *In January, the cotton fields looked bright with the white* **tufts** *ready for harvesting.*

to keep up with: to go as fast as

> *Zirimu was such a fast reader that nobody else in the class could* **keep up with** *him.*

for a moment: for a very short time

> *He looked so angry that I thought* **for a moment** *he would hit me, but he didn't.*

to pay by the pound: to pay a fixed price for each pound in weight

> *You pay for meat* **by the pound** *but for eggs by the dozen.*

to catch up with: to go faster than someone ahead so as to get near him

> *Since I was walking quickly, John had to run to* **catch up with** *me.*

row: a line of persons or things

The desks in a classroom are usually arranged in straight **rows**

Reading passage

'Come on, Joseph,' Mother said to me. 'We're going to finish picking the cotton today.'

We all took our baskets and stepped outside. It was already warm in the sun, which shone from a cloudless
5 blue sky. We climbed the short path up to our small field of cotton. The white tufts looked big and thick, and hung on the cotton bushes without moving.

'This should make a good harvest,' said Father, smiling. 'Let's begin. I'll take this first row, Mary can
10 do the next on my left, John the third row, Joseph the one after that, and Eunice can work with her mother on the next two, so that she can be taught how to do it. Now remember, everybody, to pick cleanly and carefully, and not to leave any tufts on the bushes.'
15 Each of us began the row he or she had been given. I wanted to make sure that not a single tuft was left on any bush of mine. After I had picked five bushes, I looked up to see how far the others had got. Father was several yards ahead of me already, while Mary, who
20 always picked slowly but well, was still working at her third bush. John was keeping up with father, but was working carelessly.

'Father,' I said. 'John's leaving cotton behind.'

'As usual,' said Father without stopping. 'Go back
25 and keep beside your elder brother.'

68

As I bent down again, Mother and Eunice passed me on my left. Mother was doing most of Eunice's row as well as her own.

When I reached the end of my row, I walked along the edge of the field until I came to the next one to be done. I was further ahead than anyone except Father, who had worked his way back to the other end of the field and was emptying his basket on the sheet. Mary was half-way down her row. John was sitting on the ground.

'Come on, John,' said Mother. 'You must keep working so that Father can take the cotton in for weighing this afternoon.'

John stood up. 'Here's a dead grasshopper,' he said. He looked at it for a moment and then threw it away. 'Will Father bring some sweets for us, as he did last year?' he asked.

'Perhaps,' Mother replied.

John took his basket and began working fast and carelessly again. I was just going to tell Mother, when I saw him slow down and work correctly.

As the sun rose in the sky, it became very hot in the field. Eunice went to sit in the shade of a tree. The rest of us carried on, and at midday we had finished. We stood around the sheet looking at the heap of soft white cotton.

'What a big heap!' said Mary. 'How many tufts are there in it?'

'Thousands,' I replied. 'But Father will be paid by the pound. What's the price this year, Father?'

'For this kind of cotton,' he answered, 'it's fifty cents a pound.'

That afternoon we dried and cleaned the cotton. The following morning at about nine o'clock, I helped
60 Father to tie up the sheet into a big bundle and fix it on the back of his bicycle.

'May I come with you?' I asked him.

He nodded. I got my bicycle out quickly and rode down the path to catch up with him. On the main road
65 I kept behind my father so as to tell him if any cotton began falling out.

We reached the weighing station at half-past twelve. I was feeling tired and both of us were sweating from the long ride. But when our cotton was weighed and my
70 father was given forty-one shillings, we both felt happier.

Test your understanding

1. When they began picking cotton,
   A. Mary was to the left of John.
   B. John was between Mary and his elder brother.
   C. there were two rows between Eunice and her father.
   D. John was to the left of Joseph.

2. When they began picking cotton,
   A. Joseph was working a little slower than his mother and Eunice.
   B. John was working as fast as his father, but not as well.
   C. Mary did three bushes in the time Joseph took for five.
   D. Joseph was seven yards behind his father after finishing five bushes.

3. When Joseph had finished his first row,
   A. he went to empty his basket on the sheet.
   B. Mary was further ahead than John, who was sitting down.
   C. he went to begin the seventh row in the field.
   D. he had passed his mother and Eunice.

4. John
   A. sat on the ground until Mary passed him.
   B. sometimes picked cotton correctly.
   C. threw away the dead grasshopper and stood up.
   D. went on working because his mother had told him that his father would bring some sweets.

5. Joseph's father
   A. told him that he could come to the weighing station.
   B. fixed the bundle of cotton on his bicycle by himself.
   C. rode off towards the main road before Joseph had got his bicycle out.
   D. felt tired after the long ride to the weighing station.

Answer questions in writing

1. Which were the first two rows that Joseph picked?
2. In what ways was John not a good cotton-picker?
3. Who picked cotton twice as fast as Joseph? Who picked cotton at half Joseph's speed?
4. What did Joseph's father do when he had picked two rows?
5. How many pounds of cotton had the family picked that morning?

Imagine and write

1. Imagine you are Mary. Write about how you picked cotton that morning, and what you noticed about the picking done by other people in your family.

2. Imagine you are John. Say what you did, saw, thought and felt during the morning's work.

3. Imagine you are the mother of the family. Explain how you taught Eunice to pick cotton and what you did with her when the sun became very warm.

4. Imagine you are Joseph's father. Say what happened from the time you began tying the cotton up in the sheet, until the time you were paid.

5. Imagine you are Joseph. After your father has been paid, he takes you to the house of a friend. Write about what happens there and about the journey home later in the evening.

14   NNAMUKWAYA AND THE OLD CHURCH

Before you begin reading

Study these words and expressions:

to rustle: to make the soft noise of leaves in a light wind or of a long dress as you walk

> *As I went to bed, I heard the banana leaves in the plantation begin* **rustling** *in the night wind.*

to catch fire: to begin burning

> *I held a lighted match against the paper until it* **caught fire**.

to blacken: to become black or to make black

> *The bottom of our cooking pot was* **blackened** *by the fire.*

firelight: the circle of light thrown out by a fire

> *As we walked through the village, we saw people standing in the* **firelight** *outside several huts.*

Reading passage

At sunset Nnansubuga lit the fire and put the pot over it to warm the water. Soon it would be time to cook the food for the evening meal. She sat on the ground and looked at her children playing on the compound. Little Francis was sitting near her on a mat, trying to get hold 5 of the bells around his ankles. Anna was writing with a stick in the soil at the edge of the plantation. Laurence was near Anna.

'What are you doing, Laurence?' Nnansubuga asked.

'I'm making a wheel,' replied the boy, without looking 10 up. He went on bending a straight piece of thick wire into the shape of a circle.

She noticed someone walking up the hill and then heard Stephen's greeting. It was too dark to see who it was, but she could hear that it was a woman, and that 15 her son seemed happy and excited. He came running along the path.

73

'Mother, it's Nnamukwaya. May I ask her if she will tell us a story?'

20 'Oh, please, Mother,' begged Anna, running across and kneeling near Nnansubuga.

'No,' said their mother. 'Perhaps she is tired or has come for some important business.'

Anna looked sad, but when she heard the rustling of
25 clothes behind her, she turned and greeted the old woman. As Nnamukwaya walked towards the fire, she returned the greeting warmly, and then turned to Nnansubuga.

'How are you?' she asked.

30 'Very well, thank you,' replied the mother. 'How are you?'

'I'm well,' Nnamukwaya answered. 'But my legs get very tired when I walk uphill.'

'Please sit down,' said Nnansubuga.

35 The old woman bent forward, put her hands on the ground, slowly knelt, moved one hand sideways and then sat down on the mat beside Francis.

'That's better,' she said, smiling at the little boy. 'But old Nnamukwaya can't expect to run uphill when
40 she's over seventy years old, can she?'

Stephen and Anna laughed.

'Did you run up this hill when you were a girl?' asked Anna.

'Not this hill, but one very much like it,' replied the
45 old woman. 'It is called Kalama, and one of the first churches in that part of the country was built on it. I can still remember seeing the men at work making the roof.'

Nnamukwaya became silent as she thought of those exciting times, now so far away. Stephen was trying to

74

imagine what had happened. He thought of what he 50
had seen when the new classroom building was added
to his school.

'Did they bring the bricks in big lorries?' he asked.

'Bricks?' asked Nnamukwaya, in surprise. 'Lorries?
No, no. There were no bricks then, although a few 55
years later my brother was helping to make the first
bricks in the district. Lorries came much later.'

'What was it made of, then?' asked Anna.

'Of poles, sticks and reeds,' the old woman explained.
'It was always cool inside, but rather dark too because 60
the light came in only through the big doorway at one
end of the building.'

'Is it still there?' asked Stephen.

'Oh, no,' said Nnamukwaya. 'It did not last for very
long.' 65

'Was it attacked by white ants?' asked Nnansubuga.

'No,' said Nnamukwaya. 'Two years before I was
married, it was struck by lightning, caught fire and
burnt away. Nothing was left but low heaps of ash and
a small metal cross, which was bent by the heat of the 70
fire and blackened by the smoke.'

The old woman's story made Nnansubuga remember
the meal. As she got up to put the food in to cook, she
asked Nnamukwaya to stay and have something to eat
with them. 75

'Thank you,' said Nnamukwaya. 'That is very kind
of you. While the food is cooking, I shall tell the children
a story. What shall it be about?'

The word 'story' brought Laurence across into the
firelight with his nearly finished wheel. He sat down 80
beside his elder sister.

Test your understanding

1. When Stephen greeted Nnamukwaya,
   A. Anna ran across to her mother.
   B. there was not enough light to see clearly at a distance.
   C. his mother noticed someone walking down the road.
   D. he asked her to tell them a story.

2. Anna looked sad
   A. because she heard the rustling of clothes behind her.
   B. and knelt down beside her mother.
   C. for an important reason that her mother did not know about.
   D. because she thought that Nnamukwaya would not tell them a story.

3. Nnamukwaya
   A. was greeted by all the family.
   B. was not greeted by two of Nnansubuga's children.
   C. was tired because she had often run uphill as a girl.
   D. said that little Francis was better.

4. The first church on Kalama hill
   A. was built when Nnamukwaya was a child.
   B. was built of wood and reeds and had a big door and small windows.
   C. was built of the first bricks made in that district.
   D. was too dark inside.

5. Nnansubuga remembered about the meal
   A. when Laurence came to join them.

76

B. when Nnamukwaya began the children's story.

C. because she wanted Nnamukwaya to stay.

D. because of the way the first church had ended.

Answer questions in writing

1. In what order did Nnansubuga and her children greet Nnamukwaya? Who did not greet her, and why did they not do so?

2. How far did Laurence get on with his work while Nnamukwaya was telling them about the church at Kalama? What did he do after his mother had got up, and why did he do it?

3. Why was Anna excited when she heard that Nnamukwaya was coming? Why did she become sad afterwards?

4. Later in the evening, after the meal, Nnamukwaya went home. Describe exactly how she got up from the mat.

5. Why was there nothing left of the first church at Kalama except a cross after the fire?

Imagine and write

1. Imagine you are Laurence. Say how you found the piece of wire, what you did with it, and what you listened to while Nnamukwaya was speaking. You are eight years old.

2. Write ten sentences about what your mother does when she cooks the food for an evening meal. (You do not have to describe everything she does.)

3. Imagine you are Anna. Say what you did, saw, heard

77

and felt from the time when you began writing in the soil until Nnamukwaya sat down.

4. Imagine you are Nnamukwaya, when she was young. From your home you can see the church on Kalama hill. You are standing at the door one afternoon and see that a storm is gathering near Kalama. Suddenly the lightning strikes the church. Write about what you see from your house of the burning church and the storm, and what you see when you visit Kalama hill the next morning.

5. Write eight sentences about what you see, hear, smell and feel when you are sitting near the fire after dark at your home, waiting for the evening meal.

15   NDAWULA AND THE TAXI

Before you begin reading

Study these words and expressions:

gown: a long dress usually reaching from the shoulders to the ankles

> *The Arabs were the first to wear cotton* **gowns** *in Buganda.*

to snore: to breathe roughly or noisily while sleeping

> *When my brother began to* **snore,** *I found it difficult to go to sleep.*

to draw up: to slow down and stop

> *The bus* **drew up** *outside the hospital and a lot of people got off.*

to obey: to do what has been ordered

Soldiers have to **obey** *their officers.*

I'm afraid: I'm sorry to say

I'm afraid *I can't play football this afternoon, as I've hurt my knee.*

Reading passage

When the bus drove past him without stopping, Ndawula felt first surprised and then angry. He stood in the strong sunlight and watched it disappear round a bend into the dark forest. Then he looked in the other direction along the long straight, empty road. It was ₅ really too hot to stay there. He walked back to sit under the mango tree again near Ssebunnya's shop.

'Buses usually stop here, don't they?' Ndawula called out angrily.

'Not always,' said a sleepy voice inside the shop.   10

An old man in a white gown was coming up the path from Lugala village, carrying a small bundle in one hand. He stopped outside the shop, looked at the suitcase beside Ndawula, greeted him and asked:

'Are you going to Kampala?'   15

'Yes,' replied Ndawula, 'but I don't know when I shall get there.'

'There is a bus every morning,' said the old man.

'I saw it,' said Ndawula, 'but I'm afraid the driver didn't see me. Perhaps he was sleeping.'   20

The old man frowned and turned towards the shop. 'Has the bus gone past already?'

The only reply Ssebunnya made was to snore.

'I wish I could do the same as Ssebunnya now,'
25 said Ndawula. 'But I must get to Kampala today.'

'So must I,' said the old man. 'My daughter is
expecting me and will be at the bus station.'

Ndawula looked along the straight stretch of tarmac.
A car was coming towards them very fast. He jumped
30 to his feet, picked up his case and ran to the roadside,
shouting 'Come on!'

The car suddenly steered off the tarmac and drew up
in a cloud of dust beside Ndawula. A door opened and
two women got out. While the driver took their things
35 off the roof rack and put the suitcase on, Ndawula and
the old man squeezed into the taxi.

'We are alive,' said one of the women. Ndawula
noticed that they both looked frightened and ill.

'May God protect you,' said the older woman, looking
40 back at the passengers in the car. 'After this I shall
stay at home when I miss the bus.'

In less than a minute they were rushing along through
the forest. The air was blowing in through the open
windows and Ndawula felt much cooler and happier.
45 Now he would be in time for the meeting. Just then the
car struck a hole in the road and all the passengers were
thrown in the air. Some hit their heads on the roof.

'Go slower!' shouted a man from the back. 'Do you
want to kill us?'

50 'Time is money,' said the driver, and soon they were
bumping along at seventy miles an hour again.

They passed the bus on the next hill, and left the forest
behind. Five minutes later a milestone showed Ndawula
that there were only fourteen more miles. He saw that

the car was now travelling even faster than before, at 55
nearly eighty miles an hour.

Then there was a roar beside them, and a motor-cycle
passed. A policeman was riding it and he waved his
hand to them to stop. The driver looked angry but he
obeyed. The old man was the first to get out of the taxi. 60
As soon as his feet were back on the ground, he rubbed
his sore head and said:

'Now I understand what those women meant.'

The policeman was writing in his book and asking
questions. He was not in a hurry. From someone's 65
bundle came the loud ticking of a large clock. It grew
warmer inside the car again.

'Everybody out,' ordered the policeman. 'This man
must come to the police station with me.'

They were all getting their things from the roof when 70
the old man said:

'There's the bus again.'

This time, when Ndawula waved, it stopped. There
were plenty of empty seats inside.

Test your understanding

1. Ndawula walked back to the mango tree
   A. as soon as the bus had passed him.
   B. because he was angry.
   C. because there was nothing on the road and he
   wanted to keep cool.
   D. to wait for the old man.

2. When he greeted Ndawula, the old man
   A. thought that he was in time for the bus.

B. had seen that Ssebunnya was already asleep.

C. knew he had missed the bus.

D. was standing near the edge of the tarmac.

3. The older woman

A. decided never to travel by taxi again.

B. had enjoyed the journey.

C. had decided not to take the bus that morning when she set out.

D. thought that Kampala was a dangerous place.

4. When the car struck a hole in the road,

A. it was travelling at nearly eighty miles an hour.

B. all the passengers hit their heads on the roof.

C. the driver slowed down because a passenger asked him to do so.

D. the old man hurt his head.

5. The passengers got out of the taxi

A. when it grew too warm inside.

B. because it was getting late.

C. to catch the bus.

D. when they were told to do so.

Answer questions in writing

1. While he was talking with the old man, why was Ndawula not sure when he would get to Kampala?

2. Why did Ndawula have to go to Kampala?

3. Why did the taxi stop outside Ssebunnya's shop?

4. In what ways does the passage show you that Ndawula did not like to feel hot?

5. Which of the people who came into this story did not travel in the taxi?

Imagine and write

1. You are standing near the road at the fourteenth milestone from Kampala. A cyclist stops and asks you the way to Ssebunnya's shop. He has never been on that road before. You tell him which way to go, and describe what he will see and pass through. Write what you say.

2. Imagine that you are the old man. You are at your daughter's home and you are telling her husband about the taxi journey. Write what you say to him.

3. Imagine that you are Ndawula. Say what you saw, heard and did from the time you first saw the bus coming on the long, straight road until you sat down again under the mango tree.

4. Imagine that you are the taxi-driver. Say what you saw, heard and did from the time you set off from Ssebunnya's shop until all your passengers got out.

5. Imagine you are the policeman. You chased the taxi because it was going too fast. You are at the police station giving your report to an officer. What do you tell him?

16 WANDERA AND THE TREE

Before you begin reading

Study these words and expressions:

to begin with: at the beginning

> *The runners ran very fast* **to begin with,** *but later in the race they slowed down.*

83

close to: very near

> *The cars had stopped so* **close to** *each other that it was difficult to walk between them.*

axe: a heavy knife on a long stick, used for cutting down trees

> *The farmer took his* **axe** *and went into the forest to cut some firewood from a fallen tree.*

trunk: the thickest part of a tree, between the roots and the branches

> *The workmen sawed the* **trunk** *of the fallen tree into five big pieces.*

Reading passage

When I was a boy, I lived with my parents in a hut on Kisolwe hill. I started school when I was six, and five times a week I used to walk the three miles to school with Nfugambi, my elder brother. To begin with I
5 used to sit on the bench feeling very tired for most of the day. The classroom was rather dark and often hot, and I should have fallen off the bench if two other small boys had not been sitting close to me.

I reached Class 4 without repeating, but I cannot
10 remember any of my lessons during the first three years. By then I was much stronger and usually went to school with Isingoma, who was in my class and lived close to the forest that grew around the edge of the swamp. Nfugambi had left the primary school, and I wasn't
15 sorry, as he used to walk very fast and never stopped to look at anything on the way. Isingoma was just the

opposite. Two or three times a term he and I used to be punished for coming late.

One morning, soon after beginning Class 4, we were walking through the forest looking for lizards when we heard men's voices not far away, and the sound of axes. We ran a short distance and saw two men cutting into the trunk of a very tall tree growing near the edge of the forest. Five or six others were clearing away the thick grass and bushes with long sharp knives.

'Do you think the tree will fall soon?' I asked Isingoma.

'Let's wait and see,' he replied.

We were punished again that morning at school. While we were working in the school garden, we tried to decide when the tree would fall. During the afternoon lessons I kept listening for a crash, although I knew that the men were working about two miles away. As soon as school was over for the day, Isingoma and I raced down the hill, along the road, over the river and through the plantations until we reached the forest. The men had gone, but the trunk had such a deep cut that we could not understand why it did not fall over.

While I was dressing next morning at dawn, I heard someone greet my mother outside and say:

'I have come for Wandera.' It was Isingoma.

I took my things for school and ran with him along the path past his house and into the forest, which was still cool and misty from the night. We reached the place just as the men were beginning work.

'Why don't they hurry up?' asked Isingoma.

'I'm sure it won't be long now,' I said.

One of the men cutting grass stopped and walked to

a small rock to sharpen his knife. As he was grinding
50 it, he noticed us.

'You can come and help,' he said.

Soon we were making big bundles of grass and putting
them in a heap. We enjoyed the work so much that we
forgot all about school.

55 'Look out!' shouted a man. 'It's falling your way.'

I looked up at the big tree. It was falling straight
towards me. For a second I was so frightened that I
could not move. Then I ran wildly away and threw
myself into some long, thick grass. I heard the noise of
60 tearing and crashing near me, and a wind seemed to
blow past my head. I looked up and found leaves and
branches all around me. I stood up and began climbing
through.

'Where are they?' someone said.

65 'They must be caught underneath,' said another man.

'There's one of them,' said a third, as I stood on a
big branch and looked out over the fallen tree. Two men
climbed quickly over and helped me out.

'Isingoma,' I said, looking around. 'Isingoma!' I
70 shouted.

'Here I am,' he replied. A muddy boy crawled out
from underneath a bush, and stood up.

We worked in the school garden again that morning.

Test your understanding

1. The distance
   A. from Isingoma's home to the school was more
      than three miles.

86

B. from Wandera's home to the place where the tree fell was about two miles.

C. from Wandera's home to the place where the tree fell was about one mile.

D. from Isingoma's home to Wandera's was about one mile.

2. Wandera liked walking to school with Isingoma
   A. because they both liked getting there early.
   B. better than with Nfugambi.
   C. because they always found lizards in the forest.
   D. when the forest was cool and misty.

3. The big tree
   A. fell while Isingoma and Wandera were working in the school garden.
   B. fell with a crash during afternoon lessons.
   C. was not so long as Wandera thought.
   D. began to fall when Wandera was not expecting it.

4. Wandera
   A. made his way out through the upper part of the tree.
   B. was knocked down by the tree.
   C. was caught underneath the tree and could not move.
   D. crawled out from under a bush.

5. In his first year at school, Wandera
   A. always felt tired because the classroom was hot.
   B. often fell asleep in the dark classroom.
   C. felt very tired because he had to walk fifteen miles a week.
   D. was sometimes held on the bench by the bodies pressed against his sides.

Answer questions in writing

1. Which way did Wandera go to school?

2. How long did it take the men to cut the tree down?

3. What made the two boys late on the first day? What made them late on the second day?

4. Why did Wandera do very little study during the first day when the men were in the forest?

5. Describe what happened from the time the tree began to fall, until it lay on the ground.

Imagine and write

1. Imagine you are Isingoma. Say what you did, saw, heard and felt from the time the man shouted the warning about the falling tree until you crawled out from underneath the bush.

2. Imagine you are the man who sharpened his knife on the rock. You are telling Wandera's father about the accident. Write what you say.

3. Write eight sentences about what you remember seeing or feeling inside your classroom during your first year at school.

4. Imagine you are Wandera. Your shirt was torn on one of the branches as you climbed out of the tree, and you are in the headmaster's office explaining why you are late. Isingoma is standing beside you. Write what you say.

5. Imagine you are the headmaster. Write what you said to Wandera and Isingoma after they had explained why they were late.

Before you begin reading

Study these words:

cornet: a small bag made by twisting a piece of paper into a cup with a point at the bottom

Groundnuts are often sold in paper **cornets.**

customer: a person who buys things in a shop

Shopkeepers are always glad to see **customers** *who spend a lot of money.*

cardigan: a pull-over with sleeves and with buttons down the front

As it was hot, my sister took off her **cardigan** *and put it over her head.*

handkerchief: a small square piece of cloth, usually made of cotton

I saw that the Minister had a folded white **handkerchief** *in the top pocket of his coat.*

to cheat: to do wrong secretly in order to win something for yourself

The boy **cheated** *in the examination when he opened his English book under his desk.*

Reading passage

As we walked down the path leading to the market, I saw that two women were already there. They were spreading out mats on the hard earth. Others were coming along the main road, each carrying a pot, bundle
5 or basket on her head.

When we reached the market, we went round to our usual place at the corner. On the way there my mother greeted an old woman called Nnamusoke, who was putting groundnuts out in small cornets on a reed mat
10 in front of her.

'How is your back today?' asked my mother, after the greeting was over.

The old woman looked up, smiled and said: 'No better and no worse.' As we passed on, she dug her
15 hand into the bag of groundnuts beside her.

At last I was able to lift down the heavy basket of beans. I stood resting for a short time while my mother prepared the mats. Then I knelt beside her and helped to arrange our vegetables neatly on pieces of banana
20 leaves. When we had finished, I sat back. I was sure that customers at the market would not pass us without stopping and perhaps buying something.

I had just taken off my cardigan when the first customer arrived. She looked at the beans and I could see
25 from her eyes that she was trying to see which heap was the biggest. After looking quickly at the other two kinds of vegetable we had, she bent down and began to touch the cassava carefully, as if there was a snake under it.

'It's fresh,' said my mother. 'Break a bit off and see
30 for yourself.'

After doing so, the woman knelt down and silently began putting one heap of cassava slowly into her bag. She took one piece at a time and pressed it between her fingers and thumb before putting it in. Still without speaking, she untied a blue and white handkerchief and held out twenty cents, which my mother took with both hands.

Two other women had stopped at our mats. One was very fat and pushed our first customer out of the way as she was picking up her bag.

'Those heaps of beans are small,' she said loudly to her friend and looked at me. 'Make them the right size, and perhaps I will buy one.'

'They are the usual size,' answered my mother in a clear voice. 'I have been selling vegetables in the market for two years, and no-one has ever had small heaps from me.'

'Two years!' cried out the fat woman. 'Now you listen to me. When I sold vegetables at Mityana, I gave my customers heaps twice as big as yours.' She bent down, pushed her fingers into one of our heaps and pulled out one black bean. 'I did not cheat my customers with bad beans, either.'

While my mother and the fat woman were trying to agree, I sold two heaps of maize and a pawpaw to a European. She had a beautiful blue dress on and little white shoes, but she looked hot and unhappy. As she moved away, I felt someone standing behind me. It was Nnamusoke. I looked quickly across to her mats and saw her granddaughter there. My mother explained to the old woman what the matter was.

'You used to sit near the gate, on the left, I think,' said Nnamusoke to the fat woman.

'That's right,' she replied.

'I remember your vegetables,' the old woman went
65 on. 'They were always good, and the heaps were a bit
bigger. But that was ten years ago. Nowadays everything
costs more.'

The fat woman walked away, but her friend bought
some of our beans. More customers came and for a
70 time I was quite busy. At noon my mother said:

'Elizabeth, put the maize back in your basket and
I'll carry the cassava. We have made eight shillings and
ten cents.'

I was glad that we only had two kinds of vegetable to
75 carry home.

Test your understanding

1. Elizabeth's mother
   A. arrived late at the market.
   B. went to her usual place before greeting
      Nnamusoke.
   C. was carrying a pot and a bundle.
   D. spoke with Nnamusoke before reaching her usual
      place.

2. Elizabeth's mother asked Nnamusoke
   A. about her health.
   B. about her groundnuts.
   C. when she was going back home that day.
   D. about the clothes she was wearing.

3. The first customer
   A. was difficult to please.
   B. liked talking.

C. found a snake under the cassava.

D. carefully chose the biggest heap of cassava.

4. The fat woman
   A. thought the beans were too small.
   B. wanted to buy heaps of the usual size.
   C. had sold bigger heaps at Mityana.
   D. said she would buy a heap if it was made bigger.

5. Nnamusoke made the fat woman understand
   A. that Elizabeth's mother had bigger heaps.
   B. that Elizabeth's mother had much smaller heaps.
   C. that the price of food had risen in the last ten years.
   D. that Elizabeth's mother did not cheat by giving bad beans.

Answer questions in writing

1. What vegetables did Elizabeth and her mother bring to market?

2. Describe what there was on the mats in front of Elizabeth and her mother.

3. What were the first three heaps Elizabeth and her mother sold, and who bought them?

4. How did Nnamusoke help Elizabeth's mother?

5. How much of each kind of vegetable had Elizabeth and her mother sold at noon?

Imagine and write

1. Imagine you are Nnamusoke. You set off from home before dawn that morning. Say what you saw, heard, thought and did from then until you had got all your groundnuts arranged in paper cornets.

2. Imagine that you are walking around the market. Write eight sentences about what you saw there to be sold. Describe the way the goods are arranged, and their shapes and colours.

3. Imagine you are the fat woman. You are talking to a friend the following day and telling her what happened when you tried to buy some beans. Write what you tell her.

4. Imagine you are Elizabeth. Describe the woman who bought cassava, the fat woman and the European. Use your imagination to add to what is said about them in the reading passage.

5. Think of an old woman who lives near you. Now write eight sentences to show what she looks like and to say how she spends her time during the day.

18   THE ARITHMETIC EXAM

Before you begin reading

Study these words:

classmate: a person who is in the same class as you are

Martha and Felicita were **classmates,** *but they did not often speak to each other.*

to move: to change your home from one place to another

When I was seven years old, we **moved** *from Mumias to Broderick Falls.*

Reading passage

Ssekitto felt cool as he walked to school through the morning mist. He held a ruler in one hand, and he could feel a lump in his pocket where he had put a rubber beside his pen and pencil. That morning he had not found it difficult to remember to take his school things 5 with him.

'Wasswa!' he shouted. The limping shape in the mist ahead of him turned and stopped. Ssekitto took the bottle of ink from his head and ran up to his friend. 10

'I can walk faster this morning,' said Wasswa. 'Soon my ankle will be all right again.'

'Will we be late?' asked Ssekitto, walking more slowly than usual to stay beside his friend.

'No,' replied Wasswa, looking at his watch. 'It's 15 only half-past seven. The examination doesn't begin until after eight.'

At ten minutes to eight the two boys reached the compound and joined some of their classmates standing there. Muwanga was saying his multiplication tables in 20 a loud voice, and Kiwanuka was trying to do some difficult questions from the back of the arithmetic book. Nobody was playing football or running about. Some boys were talking excitedly, while others seemed to be dumb and looked unhappy. 25

When Ssekitto walked into the classroom just after eight, he saw Mr Tamale standing at the teacher's desk. On it there was a thick packet of paper, which was open at one end, and a big envelope, which was still shut. All the boys stood silently at their desks until Mr Tamale 30

95

wished them good-morning. Then they replied to his greeting and sat down.

'First,' said the teacher, 'I shall make sure that each boy has everything he needs. Put on the desk in front 35 of you your pen, pencil, rubber and ruler.'

Ssekitto felt a push at his back. He turned round.

'I want to fill my pen,' whispered Kiwanuka. 'Lend me your ink.'

Ssekitto looked through the glass into his bottle. It 40 was still more than half full. He passed it over his shoulder, thinking that this would be the last time, as Kiwanuka's parents were moving to Masaka soon. Then he wrote his name and number on the answer sheet which the teacher had just given him.

45 At ten minutes past eight the headmaster came in and Mr Tamale opened the big envelope. The question papers were quickly given out and the headmaster gave the signal to begin. Ssekitto at once took up his pen and began answering the questions. He found the first very 50 easy, as it was only adding, but the second took a little longer to finish because he was not very good at subtraction. He looked up and saw that it was already twenty past eight. The headmaster had gone but he had written on the blackboard in yellow chalk: 8.15–9.45. 55 Ssekitto began to do the third question.

Muwanga did not finish answering the second question until half past eight. He found the next question very difficult, but he had expected this, as he had always been weak at multiplication. He did not 60 begin Number 4 until nine o'clock. At this time Kiwanuka was half-way through the last question, and Wasswa and Ssekitto were both starting Number 7.

At twenty minutes to ten, Ssekitto was working hard at the last question. It was about a man digging a square field, and he had to find out how many days the man 65 took to do it. The first answer had said that it took the man only two-fifths of a day, so he had started again, hoping to see where his mistake was.

'Time,' said Mr Tamale. Ssekitto looked in surprise at the office clock, which had been brought in and put 70 on the cupboard before the examination began. It really was time. He put his pen down sadly. He had only been able to complete eight questions.

In the compound the whole class had gathered round Kiwanuka, who was reading out the answers from a 75 small piece of paper he had brought out of the classroom.

'Last question, two and a half days,' he said.

Ssekitto suddenly understood what his mistake was.

Test your understanding

1. Ssekitto
   A. always found it easy to remember to take his things to school.
   B. held a ruler in one hand and had all his other things in his pockets.
   C. had remembered his school things without difficulty because it was an examination day.
   D. never forgot his things on misty mornings.

2. Ssekitto decided that it was Wasswa ahead of him
   A. when Wasswa turned and stopped.
   B. because of the way Wasswa was walking.

C. because Wasswa always limped.

D. and ran up to him because it was late.

3. The headmaster came into the classroom
   A. more than ten minutes after Ssekitto.
   B. twenty minutes after Mr Tamale.
   C. twenty minutes after Wasswa reached the compound.
   D. when the examination began.

4. In the examination
   A. there were ten questions in all.
   B. Muwanga spent more than half an hour on Number 3.
   C. Ssekitto worked as fast as Wasswa for the first forty-five minutes.
   D. Kiwanuka had finished half-way through the time allowed for the examination.

5. When Mr Tamale said it was time,
   A. Ssekitto did not believe him.
   B. Ssekitto had just seen where his mistake was.
   C. Muwanga was still doing Number 3.
   D. Ssekitto looked at the office clock.

Answer questions in writing

1. Kiwanuka was good at arithmetic. In what ways does the passage show you this?

2. During the examination, what was there on each boy's desk?

3. How can you show that Ssekitto did not sit at the back of the class?

4. What was the mistake that Ssekitto had made?

5. What arrangements were made in the classroom by Mr Tamale before the examination began?

Imagine and write

1. Imagine you are Wasswa. Write about your walk to school on the morning of the examination.

2. Imagine you are Kiwanuka. Write about what you did in the classroom before and during the examination, and what happened outside afterwards.

3. Imagine that you are Mr Tamale. You have just marked the papers and made out the list. Ssekitto is first, Wasswa second and Kiwanuka third. Kiwanuka has been a bit careless. Explain to the headmaster how Ssekitto has come first.

4. Imagine you are going on with the story in the reading passage, and writing it yourself. You want to let the reader know what Muwanga thought and felt about the examination. Use your imagination and write about this.

19   MAI SUNSAYE

Before you begin reading

Study these words and expressions:

sandals: shoes open at the top and fastened with a strap or straps across the foot

> *In some parts of Africa,* **sandals** *are sometimes made out of old motor-car tyres.*

gourd: round plant, made empty inside and dried, and often used for holding liquid

> *He put the* **gourd** *to his mouth and drank the beer.*

scrub: small bushes and grass growing here and there on dry land

> *After leaving the river valley, we reached a wide plain covered with* **scrub.**

injection: a way of giving medicine by pushing a needle through the skin and pressing a liquid through the needle into the body

> *Otim was given several* **injections** *to help him get better from his illness.*

He **could not believe his ears**

> *He heard something so surprising that he did not believe it.*

The reading passage which follows is taken from *Burning Grass* (published by Heinemann), a story about Northern Nigeria by Cyprian Ekwensi.

Reading passage

Mai Sunsaye kicked off his sandals, put his feet in the cool water and felt better. He bent down, keeping his clothes out of the water. He washed his arms up to the elbows and passed his wet hands over his face. He began to watch the people who were coming to the stream.   5

He first noticed two lovely Fulani maids. Their hair was newly done and their bodies were oiled. They wore copper ear-rings and as they set down their gourds of milk, a hundred shining bracelets slid smoothly down their long arms.   10

A donkey walked into the edge of the stream, carrying a load of sugar-cane. Other donkeys came, carrying yams. Sunsaye thought that today must be market day somewhere, and that if he followed these people, he would get to a market. Perhaps he might at last find   15 Jalla there. He walked along the stream until he came to a man washing out his mouth. After greeting him, Sunsaye asked him the way to the market, and the man, standing up and calling his donkey, told Sunsaye to follow him.   20

When they came to the top of the river-bank, Sunsaye looked out over the scrub and saw in the distance people hurrying from north, south and west across the dusty hills. They were walking towards some grass huts that stood on a plain about a mile away. The donkey moved   25 slowly, and people from the stream began passing Sunsaye on their way to market. The two Fulani girls were just walking past.

'Jalla! Ah, Jalla!' said one of the girls. She ran away from the other, laughing, and then stopped and turned, still smiling.

Old Sunsaye could not believe his ears. 'Did I hear you say Jalla, my pretty maids?'

The girls looked at each other in silence, and then at him, turning their heavy gourds slowly on their heads.

'We were only playing,' one of them said at last.

'All is well,' Sunsaye said. 'I am his friend.'

The darker girl then spoke. 'Yes, we were talking about Jalla.'

'Then you know him?'

'Know him?' asked the other, now coming nearer again. 'The man from whom we buy our milk and butter? Know him? Allah be praised!'

'Ah, how can an old man know all these things? I was only asking. You see, I am a stranger in these parts.'

'Wait...Jalla may even be in the market today. He must come and buy some ear-rings for....' They looked at each other and laughed.

Sunsaye's heart fell. So Jalla was married or was going to marry, and he had told no-one.

The man with the donkey was waiting some distance ahead. He had placed his stick across his shoulders and was resting his wrists over it.

'Come on,' he called impatiently.

'I'm coming,' replied Sunsaye, sadly.

'You wanted to know something about Jalla?' asked the man, striking his donkey with the stick. 'Why didn't you ask me? The man who doesn't know Jalla in these parts must really be a stranger.'

'I was only——' 60

'Well, Jalla is a friend of the Bodejo. The Bodejo is a white man, and kind. He gives injections to cattle. You understand? He says injections will keep them healthy.' The man roared with laughter.

Mai Sunsaye did not laugh. How had his son become 65 friends with the Bodejo?

Test your understanding

1. Sunsaye spoke to the man washing out his mouth
    A. since he was tired of being alone.
    B. to get some sugar-cane to eat.
    C. as he wanted to get to the market.
    D. because it was a market day.

2. When Sunsaye came to the top of the river-bank,
    A. he was able to see the market buildings.
    B. he saw people coming from every direction towards him.
    C. he saw the two Fulani girls ahead of him on the road.
    D. he saw only scrub, people and dusty hills.

3. When Sunsaye asked the girls if they had spoken of Jalla, they at first
    A. pretended they did not know Jalla.
    B. were not sure what to answer.
    C. said they were not talking about Jalla.
    D. said they were talking about Jalla.

4. Sunsaye thought that Jalla was married or was expecting to get married
   A. because he was a rich trader in milk and butter.
   B. since he was going to buy ear-rings at the market for someone.
   C. as he was going to the market to find a wife.
   D. as the girls had been talking about him.

5. The man with the donkey roared with laughter
   A. since he liked the Bodejo.
   B. as he enjoyed going to market.
   C. because he did not believe that injections kept cattle healthy.
   D. at Sunsaye because he was a stranger.

Answer questions in writing

1. What do you think made Sunsaye notice the bracelets on the arms of the Fulani girls?

2. What made Sunsaye think it was a market day?

3. Which of the two Fulani girls first replied to Sunsaye? Explain how you know this.

4. What did the man with the donkey do while Sunsaye was talking to the Fulani girls?

5. Why was Sunsaye looking for Jalla?

Imagine and write

1. Imagine you are the man with the donkey. Say what you did from the time when Sunsaye first greeted you until you laughed about the Bodejo.

2. Imagine that you are the darker Fulani girl, and say how you had prepared to come to market.

3. Write about the preparations that your father or mother makes before going to market, or before going to visit a town.

Before you begin reading

Study these words and expressions:

to go upstairs: to go up the steps leading to a higher part of a building

> *When we arrived at the Ministry, we were asked to* **go upstairs** *to see Mr Opu.*

measles: an illness that makes you feel hot and brings itchy spots out on your body

> *Many children have* **measles** *before they are ten years old.*

ceiling: the top surface of a room, usually stretching flat from wall to wall

> *The lizard crawled upside-down along the* **ceiling**, *looking for flies.*

to have fun: to enjoy yourself, usually smiling and laughing

> *Before lessons begin, we* **have fun** *playing with a ball on the school compound.*

The baby was **called Ssendegeya after his grandfather**

> *The baby was given the name Ssendegeya because that was his grandfather's name.*

It was not long before the bus appeared

> *After a short time the bus appeared.*

Read this

Here are four words you know well:

> father   mother   brother   sister

Do you know how to use them correctly? You can only have one **father**. He is the man whose seed you come from. You can only have one **mother**. She is the woman who gave birth to you. Your **brothers**
5 and **sisters** all have the same father and the same mother as you. You all have the same **parents**. A child who has the same father as you but not the same mother is called your **half-brother** or **half-sister**; so is a child with the same mother but not the same
10 father.

Your father's brothers and your mother's brothers are your **uncles**. Your father's sisters and your mother's sisters are your **aunts**. There are not two different words, one for your father's brothers and the other for
15 your mother's brothers. All are your uncles. In the same way, there is no easy way of showing the difference between your aunts. If you want to show the difference, say 'my father's brother', 'my father's sister', 'my mother's brother' or 'my mother's sister'.

106

Your father and all his brothers and sisters have one 20
father and one mother. These two persons are your
grandfather and your **grandmother**. Your mother's
father and mother are also called your grandfather and
grandmother. You have two grandfathers and two
grandmothers; you have four **grandparents**. You 25
cannot have more than four grandparents.

The woman who is married to your uncle came from
another family. But she is also called your **aunt**. The
man who is married to your father's sister or your
mother's sister came from another family. But he is 30
also your **uncle**. The children of your uncles and aunts
are called **cousins**. There are no special words to show
whether a cousin is a boy or a girl. Each is just called
a cousin.

The people in your family who are nearest to you are 35
your brothers and sisters, your father and mother, and
your grandparents. All the other people in your family
may be called your **relatives** or your **relations**. You
are **related** to them.

Answer these questions without writing

1. How many brothers and sisters have you?
2. How many of your four grandparents are still alive?
3. Which of your uncles lives nearest to your home?
4. Are any of your cousins in secondary school now?
5. Have any of your relatives ever travelled to Europe or America?

This reading passage is about the arrival of a new baby in a West African family. It is not a story that someone imagined: it really happened in Freetown in Sierra Leone about fifty years ago. If you want to, you can read more about this family in a book called *Kossoh Town Boy* (Cambridge University Press), by Robert Wellesley Cole.

Reading passage

Soon there was a third brother to join Arthur and me. There were two years between him and Arthur, who was two years younger than I. He was called Wilfred, after Father.

5   We had not known that a baby was coming, but one morning suddenly everybody was busy in the house. Both my grandmothers were there, and other women came and went. For once we were not allowed to go into our parents' rooms.

10   Then in the evening there was a new cry, the cry of a baby. We rushed upstairs, walked very quietly to mother's door and knocked. But we were still kept out. The following morning, when at last we were allowed to enter, there was a new baby lying beside mother.
15 Its skin was yellowish-brown and its eyes were not quite shut. It seemed to be watching us.

Arthur and I crept up to the bed and looked at mother and the little baby. Then we slowly stretched out our hands and touched baby's mouth, his little flat
20 nose and his forehead. He was alive. He was one of us.

Baby Wilfred soon showed that he was very much one

of us. He became the most loved person in the family. He was always smiling, and always in the middle of what was happening. Soon he went where Arthur and I 25 went and did what we did.

We liked to be together and even had measles all at the same time. To protect our eyes against damage from this illness, large white circles were drawn round our eyes with a kind of chalk. In our nature study book 30 there was a picture of an owl. When we looked at each other, we thought we looked like owls. We had great fun shouting 'Owl!' at each other.

During the rainy season, the three of us liked to hide in the dark corners of the bedrooms upstairs and listen 35 to the rain. The heavy raindrops beat noisily on the corrugated iron roof, and the space between the roof and the wooden ceiling of the bedroom made the sound even stronger. The rain seemed to be making music by drumming on our house. When a storm broke above us 40 and the thunder rumbled and crashed and the lightning struck, we children really loved it.

When Arthur learned the alphabet, baby Wilfred joined in. The alphabet and some pictures were printed on a large sheet of thick paper. The capital letters were 45 on one side and the small letters on the other. It was not long before Wilfred was able to read all the letters from A to Z. Yet he was only two years old.

I know he was only two at that time because I remember that something very sad happened in our home not long 50 after. One day the house became very silent. Big tears appeared on mother's face. Father did not leave to go to work at the office. Relatives arrived. Then it came out. Wilfred was dead.

55 He had been well the night before, but now he was gone. He had become ill suddenly during the night, and the illness had been too strong for him.

The following year, three years after Wilfred was born, a baby girl joined our family. She was the first of 60 my sisters, and was named Phoebe Winifred.

Test your understanding

1. The writer of this passage was
   A. seven years older than Phoebe Winifred.
   B. two years older than Wilfred.
   C. two years younger than Arthur.
   D. three years older than Phoebe Winifred.

2. The writer's mother gave birth to
   A. only three children.
   B. four children in all.
   C. at least five children.
   D. three boys and three girls.

3. The three boys thought they looked like owls
   A. because it was dark upstairs in the bedrooms.
   B. since owls have white eyes.
   C. as owls have large circles round their eyes.
   D. because it was great fun.

4. The noise of the rain was especially loud
   A. because it drummed on the house.
   B. although the thunder rumbled and crashed and the lightning struck.
   C. as the ceiling was made of corrugated iron.
   D. since there was an empty space between the iron roof and the wooden ceiling.

5. The large sheet of thick paper had
   A. capital letters and pictures printed on it.
   B. capital and small letters and pictures printed on it.
   C. letters on one side and pictures on the other.
   D. a picture drawn on it and two printed alphabets.

Answer questions in writing

1. What was the name of the writer's father?

2. For how long were the children kept out of their mother's room when Wilfred was born?

3. Write five sentences about Wilfred.

4. What unusual things did the writer notice on the morning after Wilfred's death?

5. Which did the children enjoy more, the noise of the rain, or the thunder and lightning? Give a reason for your answer.

Imagine and write

1. Think of a small child you know who is about two years old. Write ten sentences about what it often does.

2. Describe a game you enjoyed playing with your brothers and sisters when you were small.

3. What do you see and hear when you are in your house during a storm?

4. Write ten sentences about your family.

Before you begin reading

Study these words and expressions:

to hurl: to throw with great strength

> *The hunter* **hurled** *his spear at the antelope.*

to seize: to catch and hold firmly

> *The robber tried to escape, but the policeman* **seized** *him by the arm.*

to argue: to disagree in words

> *When a ruler was found on the classroom floor, two boys began to* **argue** *about it; each boy thought the ruler was his.*

to scramble: to walk quickly or run over a rough surface

> *When the monkeys caught sight of the lion, they* **scrambled** *away over the rocky ground.*

now and then: sometimes, but not often

> **Now and then,** *Kosaki wrote a letter to his parents.*

P.E.: physical education (exercises of the body)

> *We have* **P.E.** *at school every Tuesday morning.*

Reading passage

One hot afternoon Njoroge and Ssempa were walking home from school along the road which curved down the hill. First they passed through land covered with long grass. Then, lower down the hill, they entered plantations of banana, cotton and coffee. At a bend in the road near 5 a large, grey rock both boys stopped. In front of them they saw some other boys from their school, who were throwing sticks and stones into a big mango tree that was growing about twenty yards from the roadside.

The boys caught sight of Njoroge and Ssempa, 10 stopped for a moment, and then went on hurling small branches, pieces of rock and even lumps of hard earth up into the tree. Now and then a mango dropped to the ground. Two or three boys ran up to seize it with cries of joy, and then argued angrily about who had 15 knocked the mango down.

Njoroge and Ssempa walked quietly down the road. They hoped to pass without being noticed again. But as they were walking past, a big boy whose name was Muduku turned and called out: 20

'Come on, join in. There are plenty for us all. Or are you afraid of being caught?'

Njorogo and Ssempa knew that the mango tree belonged to a farmer called Tamutambo, whose hut lay not far away behind a banana plantation. They knew 25 too that he often passed along at this time of day. He might suddenly appear in the plantation, chase them, catch them and beat them. But the mangoes looked very juicy, and it was a hot afternoon.

Muduku ran across and took hold of Ssempa's arm. 30

'Ssempa is very good at P.E.,' he said. 'Let's lift him into the tree, and then he can shake the mangoes down for us.'

Ssempa looked worriedly at the tree. Its trunk was
35 thick and rather straight, and the lowest branch seemed a long way up from the ground. But already the other boys in Muduku's group had seized him and were pulling him to the tree. He was pushed up in the air. By standing on their hands, he was able to stretch up, get
40 his fingers round the lowest branch and lift himself up.

It was dark and cool in the thick shade. He looked outwards along the branches and saw little spots of bright blue sky between the shining green leaves. He crawled out to the end of a branch and began to shake it. He
45 heard a lot of mangoes hitting the ground below and the boys shouting as they ran to gather them up.

Suddenly there was the sound of feet running wildly away, and then a frightening silence.

'It's the chief!' Njoroge's voice came up from below.
50 'Come down quickly.'

Ssempa started to scramble back along the branch, slipped, fell through the tree and hit the ground. Leaves dropped around him, and red dust rose from the hard earth. He tried to get up, but a burning pain in his right
55 foot made him fall back again. He felt weak and ill.

The chief's car came roaring up the hill. It threw up a large red cloud behind it. It rushed past the mango tree. The chief was looking straight ahead. The wind was blowing dust all over Ssempa when he heard light
60 footsteps coming towards him. It was Njoroge.

'We're lucky,' he whispered. 'Come on, I'll help you to get away from here.'

He put his arm around Ssempa and pulled him up.
Very carefully Ssempa tried to put some weight on the
sore foot. By leaning heavily on his friend, he was able 65
to limp slowly home.

Test your understanding

1. The large grey rock was
   A. among the plantations.
   B. close to the school.
   C. near Tamutambo's hut.
   D. covered with long grass.

2. Muduku called out to Njoroge and Ssempa
   A. when they were near the large grey rock.
   B. when they were standing near him.
   C. when they were about twenty yards away.
   D. after they had walked past.

3. Ssempa looked worriedly at the tree
   A. since it was a hot afternoon.
   B. as Muduku was holding his arm.
   C. since he felt weak and ill.
   D. because he thought it might be difficult to get
      up on the lowest branch.

4. The boys ran away suddenly
   A. because they were afraid of Tamutambo.
   B. when they caught sight of the chief's car.
   C. as they had collected all the mangoes they wanted.
   D. so that Ssempa should be punished.

5. When the chief's car rushed past the mango tree,
   Njoroge
   A. was running away with Muduku.

B. was hiding somewhere near the mango tree.

C. was standing beside Ssempa.

D. was picking up the mangoes that Muduku's group had left.

Answer questions in writing

1. Were Njoroge and Ssempa day-pupils or did they board at the school? Give a reason for your answer.

2. Why could Tamutambo not see the mango tree from his hut?

3. How did Ssempa get from the ground up into the tree?

4. What shows us that Ssempa was able to make mangoes fall more quickly than Muduku and his friends had been?

5. When did Njoroge run away from the mango tree?

6. Why did Njoroge say that they were lucky?

Imagine and write

1. We do not know exactly why the boys stopped throwing sticks and stones when they caught sight of Njoroge and Ssempa. What can you think of which might have made them stop?

2. Imagine you are Ssempa. You are resting at home that evening when your father returns. He wants to know what happened. You tell him but you try to show him that it was really Muduku's fault. Write out what you say.

3. Njoroge and Ssempa did not run away when Muduku

116

spoke to them. What reasons can you think of for this?

4. Imagine that you are Njoroge. Say what you did from the time when Muduku and the others pulled Ssempa to the tree.

5. Imagine you are Muduku. Say what you did from the time when you first caught sight of Njoroge and Ssempa until you ran away.

22 BYARUHANGA PREPARES FOR SCHOOL

Before you begin reading

Study these words and expressions:

stationer: shopkeeper who sells everything you need for writing

*Joanna went to the **stationer's** to buy a packet of envelopes.*

assistant: man or woman who helps the owner of a shop to sell things

*Whenever Busawule went to Mbale, he left his **assistant** to look after the shop.*

ball-point pen: a pen with a very small metal ball at one end to write with

*Some **ball-point pens** cost less than one shilling, but they do not last long.*

fountain pen: a pen which holds ink taken from a bottle

You need a good **fountain pen** *to practise handwriting.*

nib: small pointed piece of metal for writing

If a **nib** *gets bent, it will never write well again.*

My friend Maria lives in the **house opposite** ours.

My friend Maria lives in the house nearest ours, on the other side of the street.

Reading passage

When Tinkamanyire awoke, he looked at the clock that stood near his bed on the table. The front of the clock shone in the dark and showed him that it was six o'clock. He got out of bed and walked across to where
5 Byaruhanga was sleeping.

'Wake up,' he said quietly, shaking his brother's arm. 'Wake up. We must get up and dress. The bus leaves in an hour.'

Both boys began to put on their clothes, which were
10 arranged on the table. Soon they were ready and went into the dining-room, where their mother gave them each a cup of sweet tea and some biscuits.

'Be careful when you cross the roads in the town,' she told them. 'Be polite at your uncle's, and don't
15 forget that the bus leaves the town at three o'clock.'

Byaruhanga picked up a bag and Tinkamanyire felt in his pocket to make sure that he had put the twenty shilling note there safely. Wishing their mother goodbye, they set out through the cool mist that filled the valley. When they climbed to the main road, they found the sun was shining brightly and they began to feel warmer.

One hour after getting on the bus, the boys were in the town. It was difficult to walk across the bus-park, which was crowded with people. In the streets around the bus-park it was very noisy. Lorries roared and cars hooted. Some men were mending the road with big machines. People were laughing and shouting. Loud dance music was coming from a radio in a hotel.

Half an hour later, Tinkamanyire and Byaruhanga were in Mutolere Road, where it was a little quieter. They entered a stationer's shop.

'Good morning,' said the assistant, coming out of a back room.

'Good morning,' replied Tinkamanyire. 'We want to buy a pen, three pencils, a notebook, a rubber and a bottle of ink.'

'A ball-point pen, or a fountain pen?' asked the assistant.

'Oh, a fountain pen, of course,' said Byaruhanga quickly. He had just won a place in a secondary school.

'Here's a good pen that students often buy,' said the assistant, showing the boys a blue pen and taking off the top. 'Would you like to try it?'

'Thank you,' answered Tinkamanyire. But when he tried it, the ink would not flow. Byaruhanga and the assistant also tried, but the nib just scratched the paper.

'Let's try another,' said the assistant, but the boys did not reply.

'Have you got black ink?' Byaruhanga asked instead.

'We have blue, red and green, but not black.'

In the end the boys spent only two shillings in that shop on a notebook and a rubber.

Two hundred yards along the road they found another stationer. Here they bought a black pen for five shillings
55 and a bottle of black ink.

'Can we buy three pencils for a shilling?' asked Byaruhanga.

'Easily,' replied his brother. 'But you need a hard pencil for maths and two softer pencils for writing notes.'
60 After spending a shilling on pencils at a shop opposite the first, they walked over a big hill to visit their uncle and aunt and have a meal with them. At a quarter past two they set off for the bus-park.

They arrived home at half past four. When they showed
65 their mother what they had bought, she shook her head and said:

'Yes, these things are all right, but we are spending a lot of money on your education now. The bus journey, too, has cost three shillings for each of you.'
70 'Well,' said Tinkamanyire, taking some coins from his pocket, 'we've brought back four shillings for you from the twenty shilling note we took away.'

Test your understanding

1. When the boys set out from home,
    A. they walked down into the mist that filled the valley.
    B. they could see that the sun was shining brightly on the main road.
    C. they at once climbed a hill to get to the main road.
    D. they could not see things that were far away.

2. The boys arrived in the town
   A. at about nine o'clock.
   B. at about eight o'clock.
   C. soon after dawn.
   D. one hour later.

3. The boys spent only two shillings in the first shop because
   A. they were hurrying to their uncle's house.
   B. the nib just scratched the paper.
   C. the only things that pleased them were a notebook and a rubber.
   D. the shopkeeper had no black ink.

4. The bottle of black ink cost
   A. two shillings.
   B. three shillings.
   C. four shillings.
   D. one shilling.

5. The shop where the boys bought the pencils was
   A. very near the second shop.
   B. nearer the first shop than the second.
   C. near their uncle's house.
   D. near the bus-park.

Answer questions in writing

1. What was on the table beside Tinkamanyire's bed?
2. The boys walked from the bus stop on the main road to their home in half an hour. Explain how you can show that this is the time they took.
3. Write down all the things in the passage which work by machinery.

4. What did the boys fail to find in the first shop?

5. When you finish reading the story, you are sure that Tinkamanyire is older than Byaruhanga. What are your reasons?

Imagine and write

1. We know that there are at least two rooms in the house where the boys live. There must be some other rooms too. What do you think these other rooms are used for?

2. Imagine that you are Byaruhanga. A friend in the next village wants to buy things for writing. He has also won a place at a secondary school. Give him advice about where to go in the town.

3. Imagine you are the assistant and say what happened when the boys came into your shop.

4. Imagine you are Tinkamanyire. A small sister of yours asks you if walking in the town is the same as walking near your home. What are the differences that you tell her about?

23   WATER FOR OKEMA

Before you begin reading

Study these words:

the rains: the rainy season

> *During* **the rains,** *roads are often wet and muddy.*

to lengthen: to become longer

> *Shadows* **lengthen** *as the sun goes down.*
> (In the same way: **deepen**—*to become deeper;* **ripen**—*to become ripe.*)

drought: an unusually long time without rain

> *There was such a bad* **drought** *in Kenya in 1961 that food had to be sent in lorries to some districts.*

caravan: a small house on wheels

> *Some Government officers who work in the bush live in* **caravans;** *others sometimes use rest houses.*

can: a metal container for holding and carrying liquids

> *In many African towns and villages, empty paraffin* **cans** *are used to carry water from the pump or the river.*

Reading passage

Day after day, the sun beat down on the dry land. The green grass that had grown during the rains turned yellow, then brown, and slowly disappeared. The red earth became so hard that a hoe could bite into it no more than half an inch, even when a strong man used it. 5
Cracks appeared in the soil, lengthened and deepened under the hard, hot, blue sky.

Okema looked sadly at the maize a few yards from the door of his hut. It was short and yellow and the cobs would never ripen. The long withered leaves moved a 10

123

little in the light wind. For five months they had been almost without rain.

Okema's wife came out and sat on the ground where the wide roof gave some shade from the midday sun. He could hear the child crying weakly with hunger inside the house.

'There is very little water left in the pool now,' she said in a flat, tired voice. 'We must go soon, or die.'

It was the first time she had spoken of leaving. Okema felt afraid. Where could they go to? There was drought all over East Acholi. The town? There was water there, and food, but only for those who had money.

He looked along the road and noticed a dust-cloud far away. It grew quickly. A car or lorry must be coming, since no buses ever passed that way. It had now come near enough for him to see that it was too big to be a car, yet it did not look like a lorry.

About a quarter of a mile away it stopped, and the driver got out. It was a European. Okema stood up. Something very unusual was happening.

'He must have lost his way,' said Adroa. 'You see, he's looking at a piece of paper now. That will tell him to go back.'

They saw him get in again and heard the engine roar. As the driver turned off the road, Okema noticed that it was a small dark green car pulling a hut on wheels. He was even more surprised when, instead of joining the road again, the car went on driving over the hard earth towards a low hill and stopped about a mile away near some thorn trees.

Late in the afternoon the car and the hut on wheels were still there. Okema walked across to join some other farmers who had already gathered near the car.

'That's a caravan,' Okwi was explaining to Opolot, when Okema arrived. They were looking at the hut on wheels. 'The white man lives in there with his wife and children.'

'But why has he stopped here?' asked Opolot. 'Is there something wrong with his car?'

'No,' replied Okwi. 'Perhaps he has come to look for gold or silver.'

'Or diamonds,' said Opolot.

'Will he pay us to dig for him?' asked Okema.

'I don't know,' answered Okwi. 'But I have heard that Europeans who live like this buy eggs from farmers.'

'Look,' said Opolot. 'There's another car.'

A big grey car slowed down as it passed Okema's house, and turned off the road. It bumped towards them, and a man got out from the back, carrying a thin black bag. He was dressed in a new black suit with shiny black shoes, and his white collar and light grey tie shone in the bright light. He walked straight across to the European, and Okwi listened carefully as they talked in another language.

'Who is that?' asked Opolot, after a short time.

'He's a relation of Mr Ogweng's, the Minister of Agriculture,' replied Okwi. 'They are talking about water. The European is going to make water come up from the earth and there will be enough for everyone to carry away in cans.'

'Why doesn't he come and do it near my house?' asked Okema. 'Then I could sell it and make money to pay my taxes.'

75 Opolot looked angry, but Okwi laughed. 'This water is free for everybody,' he said.

'That's right,' said the man in black, turning away from the European and speaking in the language of the district. 'This is the first of twenty water-holes we are
80 making all over East Acholi to help farmers improve their homes and their land. There will be plenty of water for all of you in a week.'

Test your understanding

1. Before the first car appeared, Okema
   A. felt sad when he saw there was little water left in the pool.
   B. felt sad because the maize was only a few yards from his hut.
   C. felt afraid of moving away from his farm.
   D. was afraid that there might not be enough food or water in the town.

2. Okema saw that the first car was pulling something behind it
   A. when the car left the road.
   B. when the car was driving across the land towards a low hill.
   C. as soon as it stopped about a quarter of a mile away.
   D. when he heard the engine roar.

3. Opolot
   A. knew as much as Okwi about the way Europeans live.
   B. reached the car before Okema.

C. was told that the European had come to look for gold or silver.

D. had come to mend the European's car.

4. The man in the new black suit
   A. spoke in two languages, but Okwi understood only one of them.
   B. could only speak two languages.
   C. used two languages that afternoon.
   D. understood two languages, but could speak only one of them.

5. The man in the new black suit
   A. was a brother of Mr Ogweng's.
   B. was the Minister of Agriculture.
   C. told the farmers that they would soon be able to carry away water in cans.
   D. agreed with Okwi.

Answer questions in writing

1. What had the drought done to the grass? What had it done to Okema's maize crop?

2. Why was Okema afraid of leaving his farm?

3. What surprised Okema when the car stopped about a quarter of a mile away? What surprised him after the driver got in again?

4. What points in the story show you that Okema was thinking of ways of getting more money?

5. How many men came by car to the place near the thorn trees, and who were they?

Imagine and write

1. Imagine you are Okwi. Your farm is not far from the thorn trees. Write about what you did, saw and heard from the time you saw the European come until Mr Ogweng's relation left.

2. Imagine you are Okema. Say what you told your wife when you got back home that evening.

3. Write about what the farmers and their wives and children did after the water came.

4. Imagine you are Adroa. Say what you did and saw when you went to sell eggs to the European the morning after he had arrived.

5. Write ten sentences about what you noticed near your home when it had been very dry for a long time.

24   OKAGBUE DIGS DEEP

Before you begin reading

Study these words:

charm: an object with magic power in it

> *He was not afraid to walk through the forest because a* **charm** *was hanging round his neck.*

medicine-man: a man with secret knowledge about spirits and how to cure illness

> *Carrying a white cock, the* **medicine-man** *danced and sang.*

bush: land covered with grass, bushes and some trees, but with no crops growing on it

The valley was all **bush,** *except for one small farm.*

top-soil: the earth on the surface, in which small plants grow

No farmer wants the rain to wash away his **top-soil.**

leopard: spotted animal shaped like a small lioness
One night last week a **leopard** *entered the village and carried off my dog.*

to chew: to break up food with the teeth so that it can be swallowed

We must **chew** *meat before we swallow it.*

This reading passage has been taken from *Things Fall Apart* (Heinemann Educational Books) by Chinua Achebe. It is a story from Nigeria before the Europeans had come. At that time people living in one part of Nigeria believed that there were bad spirits called *ogbanje* which were born again and again as weak children. Often an *ogbanje* chose to enter the children of one mother. Her children then all died without growing up into men or women. But if the special charm of the *ogbanje*, called the *iyi-uwa*, was found, then the children lived and grew up into healthy men and women. The passage has been made simpler to help you read it more easily.

Reading passage

'Where did you bury your *iyi-uwa*?' Okagbue asked Ezinma. She was nine then and had just got better after a bad illness.

'What is *iyi-uwa*?' she asked.

5 'You know what it is. You buried it in the ground somewhere so that you can die and then return to make your mother unhappy.'

Ezinma looked at her mother, whose sad eyes were fixed on her.

10 'Answer the question at once,' roared Okonkwo, who stood beside her. All the family were there and some of the neighbours too.

'Leave her to me,' the medicine-man told Okonkwo in a cool, clear voice. He turned again to Ezinma.

15 'Where did you bury your *iyi-uwa*?'

'Where they bury children,' she replied, and the crowd whispered to themselves.

'Come along then and show me the place,' said the medicine-man.

20 The crowd set out with Ezinma leading the way and Okagbue following behind her. Okonkwo came next and Ekwefi followed him. When they came to the main road, Ezinma turned left as if she was going to the stream.

'But you said it was where they bury children?' 25 asked Okagbue.

'No,' said Ezinma, and walked on. Sometimes she ran for a short distance and then stopped again suddenly. When she got to the big udala tree, Ezinma turned left into the forest and the crowd followed her. Because of 30 her size she made her way through the trees and undergrowth more quickly than her followers. She went in deeper and deeper. Then suddenly she turned round and began to walk back to the road. Everybody stood to let her pass and then followed her again in a long line. 35

'If you bring us all this way for nothing, I shall beat you,' Okonkwo said angrily.

'I have told you to let her alone,' Okagbue repeated. 'I know how to talk to them.'

Ezinma led the way back to the road, looked left and 40 right, and turned right. So they arrived home again.

'Where did you bury your *iyi-uwa*?' Okagbue asked patiently, when Ezinma finally stopped outside her father's hut.

'It is near that orange tree,' Ezinma said. 45

'Come and show me the exact place.'

'It is here,' Ezinma said when they got to the tree.

'Point at the place with your finger,' said Okagbue.

'It is here,' said Ezinma, touching the ground with her finger. 50

'Bring me a hoe,' said Okagbue.

When Ekwefi brought the hoe, he had already put aside his goatskin bag and his big cloth and was dressed only in a long, thin piece of cloth going round his body and between his legs. He set to work at once digging 55 a pit where Ezinma had shown. The neighbours sat around watching the pit becoming deeper and deeper. The dark topsoil was soon taken away and the bright red earth appeared. Okagbue worked in silence, his back shining with sweat. Okonkwo stood near the pit. He 60 asked Okagbue to come up and rest while he did some digging. But Okagbue replied that he was not tired yet.

Ekwefi went into her hut to cook yams, and Ezinma
went with her to help in preparing the vegetables.

65   Outside, the pit was now so deep that the people no
longer saw the digger. Suddenly Okagbue sprang to the
surface like a leopard.

'It is very near now,' he said. 'I have felt it.'

Everybody became excited and those who were
70 sitting jumped to their feet.

'Call your wife and child,' he said to Okonkwo. But
Ekwefi and Ezinma had heard the noise and had run out
to see what it was.

Okagbue went back into the pit. After a few more
75 hoefuls of earth he struck the *iyi-uwa*. He raised it
carefully with the hoe and threw it to the surface. Some
women ran away frightened when it was thrown.
Okagbue came out and without saying a word or even
looking at anyone, went to his goatskin bag, took out
80 two leaves and began to chew them. When he had eaten
them, he took up the *iyi-uwa* with his left hand and
began to untie it. A smooth shiny stone fell out. He
picked it up.

'Is this yours?' he asked Ezinma.

85 'Yes,' she replied. All the women shouted for joy
because Ekwefi's worries were at last ended.

Test your understanding

1. The least patient person in this story was
   A. Okagbue.
   B. Ezinma.
   C. Okonkwo.
   D. Ekwefi.

2. The people who heard Ezinma say 'Where they bury children' were
   A. Okonkwo, Okagbue and Ekwefi only.
   B. all the family.
   C. all the family, some of the neighbours and Okagbue.
   D. all the people in the village.

3. The complete journey made by Ezinma and the crowd led them
   A. deeper and deeper into the forest.
   B. along the main road, deep into the forest and back the same way.
   C. along the main road to the udala tree and back again.
   D. into the forest and then back by a different road.

4. Okagbue was not sure that he knew where the *iyi-uwa* was buried until
   A. Ezinma touched the ground with her finger.
   B. Ezinma said 'It is here'.
   C. Ezinma stopped outside her father's hut.
   D. Ezinma told him it was near the orange tree.

5. Okagbue threw the *iyi-uwa* to the surface
   A. after Okonkwo had helped him with the digging.
   B. soon after Edwefi and Ezinma had run out of the hut.
   C. while all the people were jumping to their feet.
   D. while Ekwefi was cooking yams in her hut.

Answer questions in writing

1. What are the names of (*a*) the child believed to be *ogbanje*; (*b*) the child's father; (*c*) the child's mother; (*d*) the medicine-man?

2. Why did Okagbue always speak quietly and patiently to Ezinma?

3. What things did Ezinma say which seemed to show the crowd that she was *ogbanje*?

4. After finding the *iyi-uwa*, what did Okagbue do which shows that he thought it had magic power?

5. What worries ended for Ekwefi when the *iyi-uwa* was found?

Imagine and write

1. Imagine you are one of the neighbours and describe the journey you made with Ezinma.

2. Imagine you are one of the family, and say what you saw and did while Okagbue was digging and when he found the *iyi-uwa*.

3. What do you imagine Okonkwo was thinking about when Ezinma led them all into the forest and back?

4. Imagine you are Ezinma and that you are not really *ogbanje*. Say what you thought and felt when Okagbue was asking you questions, and why you took the people out into the forest and back.